# Apollo 11: The History and Legacy of the First Moon Landing

## By Charles River Editors

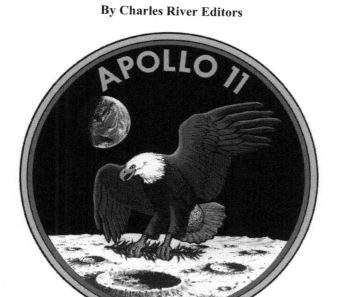

The Apollo 11 mission insignia

# About Charles River Editors

**Charles River Editors** was founded by Harvard and MIT alumni to provide superior editing and original writing services, with the expertise to create digital content for publishers across a vast range of subject matter. In addition to providing original digital content for third party publishers, Charles River Editors republishes civilization's greatest literary works, bringing them to a new generation via ebooks.

Sign up here to receive updates about free books as we publish them, and visit Our Kindle Author Page to browse today's free promotions and our most recently published Kindle titles.

# Introduction

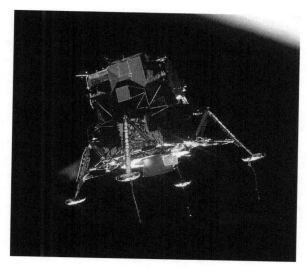

**The Eagle lunar module in the Moon's orbit**

## Apollo 11

"10, 9, ignition sequence start, 6, 5, 4, 3, 2, 1, zero. All engines running. Liftoff! We have a liftoff! Thirty-two minutes past the hour. Liftoff on Apollo 11!" Jack King, NASA Chief of Public Information

At 9:32 a.m. on July 16, 1969, time stood still throughout the world, as thousands converged on the Kennedy Space Center and millions tuned in on live television. At that instant, the first rumbles began to shake the ground, as a small spacecraft attached to the giant Saturn V rocket several hundred feet tall started lifting off. Quickly being propelled several thousand miles per hour, it takes just a few minutes to reach a speed of 15,000 miles per hour, and just a few more minutes to enter orbit at 18,000 miles per hour. Apollo 11 was on its way to a historic first landing on the Moon.

Apollo 11's trip to the Moon may have started on that day in 1969, but the journey had begun over a decade earlier as part of the Space Race between the United States and the Soviet Union. While landing on the Moon was a noble goal proposed as early as 1961 by President Kennedy, NASA and the nation as a whole moved with urgency simply to best the Soviet Union, which had spent the 1950s beating America to important space-related firsts, including launching the first satellite and cosmonaut in orbit. In fact, President Eisenhower's administration began the design for the Apollo program in 1960 in hopes of getting a head start to the Moon, despite the fact the plans originated a year before the first Russian cosmonaut, Yuri Gagarin, orbited the Earth and two years before John Glenn did.

Over the decade, NASA would spend tens of billions on the Apollo missions, the most expensive peacetime program in American history to that point, and even though Apollo 11 was only one of almost 20 Apollo missions, it was certainly the crown jewel. only one of nearly 20 Apollo missions conducted by NASA. And to make Apollo 11 a success, it would take nearly a decade of planning by government officials, hard work by NASA scientists, intense training by the astronauts, and several missions preceding Apollo 11. It also cost over $20 billion, making the Apollo program the most expensive peacetime program in American history at the time.

Americans sure felt the cost was worth it as they watched the first live shots of astronauts Neil Armstrong and Buzz Aldrin walking on the Moon. As he left his first footprint on the Moon, Armstrong transmitted one of the 20th century's most famous phrases: "That's one small step for man, one giant leap for mankind."

*Apollo 11: The History and Legacy of the First Moon Landing* comprehensively chronicles the history of the famous mission, from the initial designs to the dramatic days of July 1969 and the aftermath. Along with pictures of important people, places, and events, you will learn about the first moon landing like you never have before, in no time at all.

**Neil Armstrong about to take the first step on the Moon. Picture taken by a camera
mounted to the side of the Eagle.**

# Chapter 1: Planning Apollo

On May 25, 1961, President Kennedy addressed a joint session of Congress to discuss the importance of the Space Race within the context of the Cold War, but the speech remains famous because he spelled out his vision of landing a man on the Moon before the decade was over:

I therefore ask the Congress, above and beyond the increases I have earlier requested for space activities, to provide the funds which are needed to meet the following national goals:

"First, I believe that this nation should commit itself to achieving the goal, before this decade is out, of landing a man on the moon and returning him safely to the earth. No single space project in this period will be more impressive to mankind, or more important for the long-range exploration of space; and none will be so difficult or expensive to accomplish. We propose to accelerate the development of the appropriate lunar space craft. We propose to develop alternate liquid and solid fuel boosters, much larger than any now being developed, until certain which is superior. We propose additional funds for other engine development and for unmanned explorations--explorations which are particularly important for one purpose which this nation will never overlook: the survival of the man who first makes this daring flight. But in a very real sense, it will not be one man going to the moon--if we make this judgment affirmatively, it will be an entire nation. For all of us must work to put him there...

Let it be clear--and this is a judgment which the Members of the Congress must finally make--let it be clear that I am asking the Congress and the country to accept a firm commitment to a new course of action, a course which will last for many years and carry very heavy costs: 531 million dollars in fiscal '62--an estimated seven to nine billion dollars additional over the next five years. If we are to go only half way, or reduce our sights in the face of difficulty, in my judgment it would be better not to go at all.

Now this is a choice which this country must make, and I am confident that under the leadership of the Space Committees of the Congress, and the Appropriating Committees, that you will consider the matter carefully.

It is a most important decision that we make as a nation. But all of you have lived through the last four years and have seen the significance of space and the adventures in space, and no one can predict with certainty what the ultimate meaning will be of mastery of space.

I believe we should go to the moon. But I think every citizen of this country as well as the Members of the Congress should consider the matter carefully in making their judgment, to which we have given attention over many weeks and months, because it is a heavy burden, and there is no sense in agreeing or desiring that the United States take an affirmative position in outer space, unless we are prepared to do the work and bear the burdens to make it successful. If we are not, we should decide today and this year. "

**Kennedy's speech**

Of course, the very first issue was to figure out the best way to actually put a man on the moon. The first plan, the original plan, and the one that made the most sense, involved a direct ascent to and from the Moon. Any rocket and spaceship would launch from the Earth and travel directly to the Moon, where it would land in either an upright position or horizontally. This approach seemed feasible to NASA because the Moon had no atmosphere, making ascent from the Moon relatively easy.

When James Webb took over NASA in 1961, he inherited the agency's support for the direct ascent model. The biggest supporters of the plan were the brightest luminaries of the agency, Wernher Von Braun, the director of the Marshall Space Flight Center, and William Pickering, the head of the Jet Propulsion Laboratory. Mark Faget of the Space Task Group, who went before Congress, remembered talking to Pickering, who said, "You don't have to go into orbit; . . . you just aim at the moon and, when you get close enough, turn on the landing rockets and come straight in. . . . I thought that would be a pretty unhappy day if, when you lit up the rockets, they didn't light."[1]

**James Webb**

The plan, though risky, had plenty of support outside of NASA, and given the attention, direct ascent had the best chance of being chosen. The Air Force developed a plan and suggested its adoption, calling it LUNEX,[2] and though that plan was not chosen, the development of rockets for direct ascent began. Landing astronauts on the Moon required large rockets, much bigger in size than the Redstones and Atlases the U.S. already possessed and which had been used for Project Mercury. NASA proposed NOVA, gigantic rockets that could make the trip to the Moon.

[1] _Chariots for Apollo, Ch3-2 (Lunar Proposals: Before and After 1961)_; Maxime A. Faget, interview, Houston, 15 Dec. 1969; Ivan D. Ertel, notes on Caldwell C. Johnson interview, 10 March 1966. See also John M. Logsdon, "Selecting the Way to the Moon: The Choice of the Lunar Orbital Rendezvous Mode," Aerospace Historian 18, no. 2 (June 1971): 63-70.

[2] _Space Systems Division, Air Force Systems Command_, "Lunar Expedition Plan: LUNEX," 1961.

Though the design of the NOVA rockets looked different from other designs, the rockets belonged in the Saturn rocket family, but NOVA was intended to be much larger than the Saturn V.[3] With NOVA, the larger Saturn rocket program, and the first steps of the manned project, the price for a landing was believed to be $7.5 billion, an estimate that depended on the success of the giant rockets to land astronauts on the Moon in one single launch.

Wernher Von Braun, the former Nazi rocket scientist, did not wholly believe in the ability of direct ascent, and he made plans to land Americans on the Moon via another proposal, the Earth Orbit Rendezvous.[4] Von Braun worked with the U.S. Army to sell the idea, saying it was possible with Earth Orbit Rendezvous to establish a military base on the Moon and thus capture the strategic "high ground." But the reasons for Von Braun's proposal were much closer to his original ambitions; he viewed the Moon as a step towards the ultimate goal, a manned landing on Mars by the year 1980. Von Braun imagined fleets of spacecraft, built from successive launches

---

[3] "Nova," Encyclopedia Astronautica.

[4] "Lunar Module 2 (Earth Orbit Rendezvous)" Smithsonian, Air and Space Museum; "Lunar Module 2 (Earth Orbit Rendezvous)" Smithsonian, Air and Space Museum

of rockets from the Earth, where smaller craft combined to assemble a larger ship. It would reduce the size of the needed rockets and the plan seemed much more realistic.

**Von Braun and Kennedy in 1963**

Von Braun's plan had an immediate effect on the Saturn program, as the Army Ballistic Missile Agency, which Von Braun was closely affiliated with, endorsed Saturn. That agency reported that "if a manned lunar landing and return is desired before the 1970's, the SATURN vehicle is the only booster system presently under consideration with the capability to accomplish this mission."[5] More than anything, Von Braun's endorsement of Earth Orbit

---

[5] Army Ballistic Missile Agency, "A Lunar Exploration Based upon Saturn-Boosted Systems," ABMA Kept. DV-

Rendezvous meant Saturn, and not the larger NOVA, would be the rocket to take astronauts to the Moon. Even still, the Earth Orbit Rendezvous required the creation of a successful system of launching multiple rockets to orbit the Earth, then assembling the payload of spacecraft into one space system, for missions from low-earth orbit into deep space. Project Mercury had not tested these technologies. Success meant a new space project would need to be created. What happened was not a linear development, but a choice between two projects: Gemini and Apollo. Both plans had the potential to land on the Moon using Earth Orbit Rendezvous.[6]

While Von Braun and his team at Marshall used Gemini for the study of Earth Orbit Rendezvous, another orbital plan surfaced, and it was one that was eventually adopted by Apollo. Lunar Orbit Rendezvous, where spacecraft would assemble in the Moon's orbit, was considered due to the absence of large rocket boosters in NASA's inventory. In recognition of this problem, as early as 1959, it was suggested that spacecraft could assemble on the surface of the Moon. A lot of imagination about lunar exploration seemed to gravitate towards some kind of assemblage of craft in the vicinity of the Moon. There were plans to dock and fuel two spacecraft en route to the Moon, and even a plan to send an astronaut on a one-way trip until the later rocket could be launched to the Moon, where an automated return craft would land. In the case of either plan, what had become apparent was NASA was willing to consider another plan. One or more spacecraft would approach the moon, and, with each stage of the mission, one part after another would be discarded until the mission was accomplished and the crew could return home.

The advantages of Lunar Orbit Rendezvous did not originate with one person but several, and it was an idea that was not immediately taken seriously. That isn't too surprising given the nascent stage of the U.S. space program, which had not yet attempted to rendezvous any spacecraft in earth-orbit. As early as 1958, the Vought Astronautics Group had created plans for lunar-orbit and issued the plan to NASA as the Manned Lunar Landing and Return. This was not the first time that NASA heard and ignored the Lunar Orbit Rendezvous. At the Langley Research Center, Dr. John C. Houbolt fostered and promoted LOR to NASA. Nevertheless, the idea profoundly affected the Apollo program, and LOR would eventually dictate the future design of a separate command and lunar module, but it was never be taken seriously until Von Braun and his Marshall team endorsed the plan.[7]

## Chapter 2: Designs

The companies that built each of the launch technologies epitomized the grand vision of a federal government and American public committed to funding gargantuan budgets that would send men on their way to the Moon. Each piece of hardware that would be used for a Moon

TR-2-60, 1 Feb. 1960, pp. 224-40.
[6] *Chariots for Apollo*, Ch3-2 (Lunar Proposals: Before and After 1961)
[7] "The Rendezvous that was Almost Missed,"
http://www.nasa.gov/centers/langley/news/factsheets/Rendezvous.html; "Forgotten Engineer was Key to Space Race Success," http://hamptonroads.com/2009/11/forgotten-engineer-was-key-space-race-success

mission, from the spacecraft, to the rockets, to the assembly buildings, transports, and operations headquarters, all developed into mammoth constructions. The crawler at the Saturn V rocket's base, "a great red-white-and-black skyscraper coming to life and advancing," transported the rocket to the launch pad, but essentially it was a launch pad that moved: Craig Nelson explained in *Rocket Men*:

> "As built by (Ohio's) Marion Power Shovel Company, the crawler took shape with eight tracks, each even by forty-one feet, with cleats like a Sherman tank, except that each cleat weighed a ton. Mounter over these eight tracks was the platform, bigger than a baseball diamond, on which the Apollo-Saturn V and it mobile launcher would ride VAB [Vehicle Assembly Building] to pad one mile per hour. The package weighed nine thousand tons, two-thirds cargo, one-third crawler."[8]

---

[8] *Rocket Men*, 3.

**Saturn V on the launchpad**

12,000 corporations came from the U.S., making up a total of 400,000 employees. Boeing built the Saturn V's behemoth bottom stage in New Orleans and barged the rocket across the Gulf of Mexico and across the canals of Florida. North American Rockwell in Seal Beach, California built Stage 2, which traveled through the Panama Canal. Stage 3 was built by Douglas in Sacramento, California, and was transported on Aero Supplies' specially modified Boeing Stratocruiser -- the "Super Guppy" -- to Kennedy Space Center. This same plane would carry the Command and Service Modules from North American's Downey, California plant, while the Lunar Module traveled by train from Grumman's factory in Bethpage, New York.[9]

---

[9] *Rocket Men*, 4.

The operation to build a Saturn rocket and put a spacecraft atop it involved the individual check of every part, and the manual for these checks surpassed 30,000 pages. Every machine was "tortured" in tests to produce 99.9% reliability. If the tests worked for every dial, switch, pump, light, fan, valve, and motor, Cape Canaveral could then return to its 1,700-page control plan. 300 pounds of monomethylhydrazine and nitrogen tetroxide were loaded into the Command and Lunar Modules, and by the time it was fully loaded for launch, the rocket and spacecraft weighed around 6.5 million pounds. Nelson notes, "6 million pounds of that weight was fuel and propellant: liquid oxygen (LOX) and kerosene for stage one; LOX and liquid hydrogen (LH2) for stage 2; and the hypergolics [self-igniting] for the tiny modules that in its final days would be the missions only spaceships."[10]

Despite the fact America's history of rockets, such as the Redstone and Titan, included notorious explosions on the launch pad, not a single Saturn ever blew up. That's made all the more remarkable by the size, volume, and danger involved. As Kennedy rocket scientist Bob Jone explained, "You remained on the pad while the LOX prechilled, with xenon lights, and the wind blowing, and as those pipes chill, they scream...This thing is groaning and moaning and the hydraulic pumps are coming on...We would watch that thing ignite a beautiful, absolute, thunderous roar, zillions of horsepower, and you visualize them valves workin' and them turbo pumps goin' ch-ch-ch-ch-ch-ch. The thing if smokin' and ventin' and shakin' and screamin'!"[11]

Apollo would carry men to the Moon partly because of the success of the Saturn. The rocket design signaled the intersection of a great many ideas about the future of American spaceflight and what kind of agency NASA would be. The short answer is civilian. Gemini used a military rocket, the Titan IIA, a heavy booster. The U.S. Air Force also had their hands all over the rocket, using it to launch spy satellites, and the military branch also planned to use Gemini, or Code Blue, as the missions would have been called. Military astronauts would have flown Geminis (I, II, and "Big Gemini") and docked them with Air Force spy space stations, demonstrating just how much the Cold War mentality already infected much of the U.S. space program. While there was the "Space Race," there was also the Rocket and Missile Race, and that larger competition between nations, which also involved a great deal of the same technology, signaled to some the growing danger of the militarization of outer space.[12]

There was not only a competition between nations, but one between American rocket and missile scientists as well. The debate about what to do with space, either to extend the arms race into Earth orbit or let the scientists have their way, preoccupied the decision-making of President Eisenhower. On the eve of leaving the office of the presidency, he was faced with a decision to cancel the Mercury Program and not initiate a replacement. Advisors warned him of the "scientists," saying if he allowed men like Wernher Von Braun to control the space program,

---

[10] *Rocket Men*, 6-7.
[11] *Rocket Men*, 6.
[12] *Rocket Men*, 90.

scientists would want to explore the solar system.

Eisenhower never made a decision, instead leaving it to Kennedy and his administration to chart a course for the direction of the Moon program.[13] It can be said, in some important regards, that the seeds of the Apollo programs began because of the accelerating pace of the arms race during the Cold War. The race to develop better missiles, the context of the Space Race, actually led the Soviet premier Nikita Khrushchev to place missiles in Cuba. It was with future American disasters on the island nation, first at the Bay of Pigs, then the Cuban Missile Crisis, that Kennedy stepped out of the shadow of the military leaders in the Pentagon and decided that the Space Race -- especially America's place in the contest -- had another dimension, the human element and its effect on the whole of humanity.

All at once, events fell into place that supported Kennedy's decision to enlarge the civilian sector in NASA. The effect of Alan Shepard's mission into space showed Kennedy the importance of the public's interest, and the president realized the public's imagination and participation was just as important, if not more, than the presence of the military in the space program.

Kennedy's administration also played a role in expanding his idea about the importance of a Moon mission to American society, and how civilian life could be positively affected if allowed to participate. While Defense Secretary Robert McNamara predicted that a Moon mission would have an economic effect on the national aeronautics industry, it was the influence of vice-president Lyndon Johnson that turned Apollo into the mainstay of the civilian-led space program that NASA was to become.[14] Johnson's support for the civilian sector in NASA was what led to his embrace of the Apollo program.

There are a number of ways to look at Johnson's support for the civilian role in the space program, some of which take the line that the Soviet's successes with early space launchers demanded a counter by a 'free, democratic people.'[15] A militarized space program did not share into the narrative of "liberty." Historians and journalists have also remarked upon Johnson's support for the "Southern High Technology Crescent"[16], the notion that Johnson wanted to develop Southern colleges and universities. The Apollo Program, with technicians, engineers, and scientists from Southern schools, could serve as a goal for the first graduate classes, and a fully-realized space program with the best professionalized civilian corps could accomplish a great deal towards the promulgation of American entrepreneurship and craftsmanship beyond the Earth. Space craft companies could hire American civilians from not just one but many American aerospace companies, which Johnson's 'Southern sons' might have enjoyed.

---

[13] *Rocket Men*, 139.

[14] *Rocket Men*, 155, 157, 159.

[15] *Rocket Men*, 132.

[16] "By Gemini to the Moon," http://www.astronautix.com/articles/bygemoon.htm

When the idea came to pick between Earth Orbit Rendezvous (EOR) or Lunar Orbit Rendezvous (LOR), it was the matter of creating a separate Moon lander that settled the issue. North American had been granted the contract to build what would become Apollo's Command Module; and they proposed cutting the crew to two astronauts, with the promise that Direct Ascent could then be accomplished. This plan seemed to solve the matter of risk between EOR and LOR, but Direct Ascent also would have made North American the only builder of the spacecraft.[17] But by this time, the Apollo program had gone far beyond the plans of Gemini, and even its own creators. LOR would be chosen, and the two spacecraft design of Apollo would be the choice, as Gemini, which still fit within the plan of Direct Ascent, fell to the wayside. Apollo's ambitiousness meant more glory, and contracts, for American aerospace companies; the promise to build a lunar craft would expand an industry, one already in full-swing. The public's attention to the Space Program had waned during Gemini; while Apollo ambitiousness not only promised to expand America's aerospace economic infrastructure but also potentially capture the public's imagination with moon bases, extensive lunar expeditions, space stations, and missions to Venus.[18]

Perhaps Gemini succeeded too well at its original mission, training astronauts for Extra Vehicular Activities (EVAs) and docking rendezvous, to ever have a chance to supplant the more ambitious Apollo. But Gemini did one thing amazingly well by serving as a real-time, real-life training simulator for astronauts to embark on a Moon mission. The pilots who trained with the spacecraft learned valuable lessons that were immediately put into practice with Apollo.

## Chapter 3: Crews

Assembling the crews for Apollo together, and especially the men who would land on the Moon, required combining talents and individuals who could fulfill every complex task along the way. The U.S. space program had begun with military test pilots who became astronauts, and training the astronauts for a lunar mission continued the same grueling tasks. [19] Nelson wrote in *Rocket Men*, "'Overtraining' barely described Apollo 11's punishing workload. besides all the astronauts spending fourteen-hour days in the Houston simulators learning everything that could possibly go wrong with machines and their ground controllers, Collins also had a docking simulator at Langley, Virginia, to fly; space suits in Delaware to test; and 10 gs of centrifuge to overcome...Each would-be astronaut was monitored by doctors who tested his response to the stress of ahd decelerations and up to 15 gs of force, pressure that flattened eyeballs and burst capillaries."[20]

[17] *Rocket Men*, 209.

[18] "What if NASA's Apollo Program Had Not Been Canceled?"
http://www.scientificamerican.com/article.cfm?id=what-if-nasas-apollo-program ; "Before the Fire: Saturn- Apollo Applications (1966)," http://www.wired.com/wiredscience/2012/08/before-the-fire/ ;
[19] *Rocket Men*, 33.
[20] Rocket Men, 59.

Other factors that Apollo astronauts shared with their predecessors were educational and professional backgrounds in engineering.[21] NASA had meant to train astronauts for every single contingency the mission might face, and every astronaut who would go to the Moon also engineered some part of the hardware. Astronauts took part in the process of designing, building, and testing every part of Apollo machinery, meaning each astronaut was an expert, more or less, at some aspect of spaceflight.[22] On Apollo 11, each astronaut personally played a role in the first mission to land a person on the Moon, and they were instrumental in the technical plans of a lunar landing. They had proved to be the best in their field.

Edwin Eugene Aldrin, Jr, (b. January 20, 1930) known by most as Buzz Aldrin, represented the solution that NASA used to face the challenges of a lunar mission. His choice as an astronaut for a Moon mission was more about his technical contributions to the young field of astronautics, and he was very much a military man. Aldrin graduated from West Point in 1951, flew combat missions in F-86s during the Korean War, and worked with more jet fighters for the U.S. Air Force. But ultimately, it was with his Bachelors in Science in Mechanical Engineering, and later, his doctorate in Astronautics from the Massachusetts Institute of Technology, that NASA needed. While NASA rejected Aldrin's application for the astronaut corps when he applied for the Gemini program, his dissertation, "Line-of-sight guidance techniques for manned orbital rendezvous", demonstrated to NASA that Aldrin had the intellectual vision to be an astronaut.[23] He was, after all, the first to ever receive a doctorate in astronautics. This proved enough for the complicated task of a lunar landing. Despite never being a test pilot, Aldrin was chosen as part of the Third Astronaut Class.[24] Aldrin's dissertation also demonstrated his passion, as the dedication of his thesis in January 1963, put it: "In the hopes that this work may in some way contribute to their exploration of space, this is dedicated to the crew members of this country's present and future manned space programs. If only I could join them in their exciting endeavors!"

---

[21] *Rocket Men*, 35.

[22] *Rocket Men*, 30.

[23] Line of sight guidance techniques for manned orbital rendezvous

[24] http://www.jsc.nasa.gov/Bios/htmlbios/aldrin-b.html

**Aldrin**

The inclusion of Aldrin in the astronaut corps signaled a new direction for NASA's planning. While NASA had included engineers before, key among them Gus Grissom, the inclusion of Aldrin into the corps was a recognition of the giant leap NASA must undertake to make a Moon landing successful. At this point, the American space agency was undecided on the plan to reach the Moon. Would it be an Earth Orbit Rendezvous between spacecraft, or would it take place in Lunar Orbit? In 1963, NASA could have gone either way, and even Direct Ascent was not out of the picture yet. NASA realized they had not pulled off any orbital rendezvous at all between spacecraft, and Aldrin was picked in order to make the docking between craft a very real possibility, regardless of the location of the rendezvous.

Aldrin discovered during the writing of his astronautical thesis something he called the "orbital paradox", and his discovery proved to be a formative step in the direction of a successful moon mission: "If you're trying to pilot your orbiting spaceship to reach a spaceship in a higher orbit, the intuitive course is to (1) aim your spacecraft up, towards the higher orbit, and (2) speed up your spacecraft so it will catch up. Dr. Aldrin describes the surprising result of this maneuver. You'll 'end up in an even higher orbit, traveling at a slower speed and watching the second craft fly off into the distance.'"[25]

Aldrin's genius was coming up with a way to train astronauts to dock with a spacecraft using direct observation of the target vehicle. This line-of-sight method would not be done alone; the pilot would use their direct visuals to complement and augment the computers on board the spaceship. Navigation would be a two-part act between man and machine, but Aldrin felt the combination not only made orbital rendezvous easier but also allowed astronauts to actually pilot the craft. Aldrin intended to train astronauts to ignore their "intuitions as fighter pilots" in space, "a world of three dimensions" where "there was no up and down." They should be able to manually fly their craft and dock with another during a Moon mission, even in an emergency without help from a computer.

Aldrin's intent to train an astronaut to manually fly the craft was more in line with the endless disagreements between the engineers and the astronauts. "There will forever be disagreements over who, exactly, flies NASA ships -- the engineers on the ground, or the spacemen in the capsules. Later in life, as most of his colleagues continued to claim the pilot role, Aldrin sided with the engineers: 'Gemini and Apollo were computerized and pre-planned, so the era of the pilot in command, having the creativity to decide what he wants to do -- that's gone. Only in an emergency is it apparent. And in an emergency, like Apollo 13, they had no idea what went wrong. It was like, 'We have a problem, all the lights are comin' on!' And it was up to the ground to figure out what the problem was'"[26]

If Aldrin appeared to side with the engineers, he didn't have the chance to act like one during Gemini 12, when he and James Lovell launched into space on a 4-day mission in 1966. In addition to performing a 5 ½ hour spacewalk, necessary for any moon mission that involved two spacecraft, Aldrin was forced to manually dock the Gemini spacecraft with the Agena docking vehicle.[27] Without the targeting, it was left up to Aldrin to perform what he had originally designed: the successful training of an astronaut to pilot a craft in conjunction with a computer and navigational charts. Aldrin, in a sense, stood somewhere between the engineers and the astronauts, both of whom "honored" his obsession with orbital rendezvous with the moniker "Dr. Rendezvous."[28] Nelson noted, "As an astronaut, Aldrin revealed both his smarts and his

[25] Dr. Buzz Aldrin and the Orbital Rendezvous

[26] Rocket Men, 243.

[27] NASA, Biographical Data, "Edwin Buzz Aldrin", http://www.jsc.nasa.gov/Bios/htmlbios/aldrin-b.html

[28] "Dr. Buzz Aldrin and the Orbital Paradox," http://tranquilitybaseblog.blogspot.com/2012/12/dr-buzz-aldrin-and-

simultaneous lack thereof in promulgating his MIT studies so assiduously and his opinions so stubbornly that it annoyed many of his colleagues. 'His doctoral thesis on space rendezvous...made him, in his own eyes, one of the world's leading experts,' flight director Chris Kraft said. 'Before long, the real experts...were calling him, with a touch of sarcasm, 'Dr. Rendezvous.'"[29]

Ironically, Aldrin's authorship of orbiting rendezvous would make the Gemini Program successful. Gemini has long been considered a mixed bag, but it did what it had to do. First and foremost, it showed that orbital docking between two craft could be achieved, or at the very least, it showed the U.S. could achieve this feat (the Soviets had also proved to be successful at this space endeavor). Second, it settled once and for all that orbital rendezvous, at least in Earth orbit, could be attempted and completed. By orbiting around the Earth, Gemini almost accomplished something that had never been intended; it very nearly made the Apollo Program and the idea of LOR redundant. For a brief time, the idea of EOR seemed to work just fine, and at one point Gemini was seen as the craft to get Americans to the Moon first.

Gemini was referred to as "Mercury Mark II" upon inception, but the program always had an initial identity that differentiated the spacecraft from Mercury. From the beginning, James Chamberlin and the manufacturer of Gemini, McDonnell Aircraft, considered Gemini as a viable option and competitor to the Apollo program that could accomplish a Moon landing at just 5% of the cost. They also thought Gemini could get men to the moon by 1966. Gemini would take advantage of the work on the Saturn (C) rocket, which in early 1960 was seen as one part of the larger vehicle for a Direct Ascent. Gemini took life as a docking craft, and then it evolved into a fleet of craft to dock with "trans-stage target vehicles" (upper stage Centaur rockets) to accomplish lunar flybys. Here was one proposed schedule for Gemini:

| Date | Flight | Description |
|----------|----------|----------------------|
| Mar 1964 | Gemini 1 | Unmanned orbital |
| May 1964 | Gemini 2 | Manned orbital |
| Jun 1964 | Gemini 3 | 7-day manned orbital |
| Aug 1964 | Gemini 4 | 14-day manned orbital |

orbital-paradox.html
[29] *Rocket Men*, 46.

| Sep 1964 | Gemini 5 | Agena docking |
|---|---|---|
| Nov 1964 | Gemini 6 | Agena docking |
| Dec 1964 | Gemini 7 | Agena docking |
| Feb 1965 | Gemini 8 | Centaur docking, boost to high Earth orbit |
| Mar 1965 | Gemini 9 | Centaur docking, boost to high Earth orbit |
| May 1965 | Gemini 10 | LM docking |
| Jun 1965 | Gemini 11 | LM docking |
| Jul 1965 | Gemini 12 | LM docking |
| Sep 1965 | Gemini 13 | Centaur docking, boost to Lunar flyby |
| Oct 1965 | Gemini 14 | Centaur docking, boost to Lunar flyby |
| | | |
| *Saturn C-3 Launches* | | |
| | | |

| Nov 1965 | Gemini 15 | Manned Lunar orbital |
|----------|-----------|----------------------|
| Jan 1966 | Gemini 16 | Manned Lunar landing |

Eventually, Chamberlin attempted to combine Gemini with the Apollo program in order to take advantage of the successes with the Saturn rocket. Gemini II was always billed as a possible Direct Ascent craft that could land on the Moon as a capsule with retrograde stage, upper stage ascent module, and foldable landing legs. The options to use different modules with "advanced" Gemini envisioned a fleet of craft -- "Big Gemini" -- that could rendezvous with space stations, ferry passengers from low to high orbits, and even provide a lifeboat and rescue craft for Moon explorers. To Chamberlin and McDonnell Aircraft, Gemini was the modular craft that NASA could use for years to stake a hold in Earth orbit and on the surface of the Moon.[30]

Gemini's potential never overcame the vision that Apollo encapsulated in a design that allowed the engineers to develop visionary craft to undertake LOR -- which NASA grew increasingly fond of -- and work with a large booster, the Saturn V (C-5) that promised to launch even more ambitious spacecraft than Gemini could. As a government project, the Apollo program was unrivaled and even considered a logical successor to the Manhattan Project, with the engineering and government assisted programs and agencies the program created and supported over the decade.[31] As Nelson put it in *Rocket Men*, "In so many ways, the race to the Moon would turn out to be a sequel to its predecessor's race for atomic mastery. Bother were enormous projects that only a great nation, on a federal level, could afford to attempt, and achieve. Both began with Third Reich émigrés, and a shared geography [New Mexico]."[32]

With the view of Gemini as mostly a "trainer" for U.S. astronauts, the narrative of men who traveled to the Moon makes sense and, upon first impression, follows a logical pattern. From the years 1965-1966, nine successive launches took place, and every Apollo astronaut rode on a Gemini spacecraft and participated in an ambitious schedule of experiments, maneuvers, and assessment of technology. During this time, EOR was the "cradle" for the plan to rendezvous two craft in space, and Gemini's astronauts took part in those missions. The program had started as a spacecraft designed to take advantage of the lessons from the Mercury Program, but also, and quite purposely, being built by astronauts with higher degrees in mechanical and

---

[30] "By Gemini to the Moon," http://www.astronautix.com/articles/bygemoon.htm ; "Gemini on the Moon," http://www.wired.com/wiredscience/2012/05/gemini-on-the-moon-1962/
[31] *Rocket Men*, 36.
[32] *Rocket Men*, 36.

aeronautical engineering. As each of Gemini's names represented the different intentions behind the program, such as "Mercury Mark II" meant to suggest its replacement of the first space capsule, the name "Gus Mobile" informed people in joking terms that Virgil Ivan Grissom, better known as Gus Grissom, had designed the spacecraft for astronauts to be more than passengers. Gemini taught astronauts how to *fly* in Earth-orbit.[33]

Neil A. Armstrong (August 5, 1930 – August 25, 2012) got his bachelor's degree in aeronautical engineering and master's in aerospace engineering, which gave him the solid foundation he would need to contribute to the U.S. space program. He did so immediately by joining the National Advisory Council for Aeronautics (NACA) from 1949-1952.[34] He took the knowledge he gained as a naval aviator to NASA's "High Speed Flight Station." In the spot that was to become the Dryden Flight Research Station, Armstrong flew 200 models of experimental aircraft over the Mojave Desert, including jets, rockets, helicopters, and gliders. He even test piloted the 4000 mph X-15 and the Dyna-Soar, the Air Force's attempt at a winged suborbital spacecraft.[35] Armstrong explained, "I did a lot of different test programs in those days. That was the first time I ever flew supersonic. We had two B-29s that were sued for dropping rocket aircraft, the X-1s and the Skyrockets. So I, either as the right-seat or the left-seat guy in the B-29, launched over one hundred rocket airplanes in the fifties."[36]

[33] "Gemini: 1965-1966," http://www.spacecollection.info/us_gemini/gemini.html;

[34] "Neil A. Armstrong," Biographical Data, http://www.jsc.nasa.gov/Bios/htmlbios/armstrong-na.html

[35] "Farewell Neil Armstrong: The Ultimate Test Pilot," http://www.wired.com/wiredscience/2012/08/neil-armstrong_test-pliot/

[36] *Rocket Men*, 51.

**Neil Armstrong**

While fellow astronauts would later comment that Armstrong was viewed as the "weakest" on the "[steering] stick," Armstrong came to the astronaut corps in 1962 with multiple levels of experience. His flight-time with diverse craft not only allowed him to handle different engineering characteristics but also gave him moments to work through unexpected malfunctions and other non-operable problems. "Inside the small world of military aviation, his exploits as a test pilot are still spoken of with awe. One of the stories that is told is that after landing a plane in the desert after its engines had both failed, Armstrong was rolling to a stop when he saw an obstacle that he was about to crash into. According to the legend, he used his speed and the flaps and rudders of his aircraft to force the plane up onto one wheel and, like a movie stunt driver, swerved around the obstacle precariously balanced on a single bit of rubber."[37]

---

[37] "Buzz Aldrin: Neil Armstrong Was the 'Best Pilot I Ever Knew,'"
http://www.thedailybeast.com/articles/2012/08/27/buzz-aldrin-neil-armstrong-was-the-best-pilot-i-ever-knew.html

Mechanical challenges forced Armstrong to think quick, make rapid decisions, and possess the coolness and acumen to take control of an aircraft. His colleagues recognized his skills in those regards quickly.[38] After Armstrong's death in 2012, Buzz Aldrin called him the "best pilot I ever knew." An article in *The Daily Beast* noted, "His skill as a research and test pilot certainly impressed Buzz Aldrin...Aldrin said in an interview with The Daily Beast shortly after his former colleague's death. That is high praise indeed coming from a man who had flown F-86 jet fighters in combat in Korea and who has his own impressive set of flying and technical academic credentials. Armstrong's ability to memorize the smallest engineering detail and to be able to explain, in even more detail, the intricate working of any aircraft he tested made him the outstanding test pilot of his generation. To this day, within military aviation, he is famous for his "steel trap" mind and his unflappable demeanor."[39]

After his arrival with the second class of NASA astronauts, Armstrong flew on Gemini VIII in 1966 as the command pilot. It would be Gemini's sixth manned flight, but the first to dock two spacecraft. Along with his pilot, David R. Scott, Armstrong would dock the Gemini capsule with a Gemini Agena Target Vehicle (GATV). The launch of both spacecraft went flawlessly, and the docking commenced without a hitch. Aided by computers and navigation software, as well as Aldrin's "training for orbital rendezvous", Armstrong was the first astronaut to pilot a craft and dock it with another spacecraft.

For 27 minutes, the mission proceeded as planned. Scott prepared for a two hour spacewalk, partly in preparation for expectation of EOR and the training for a lunar mission. Suddenly, both spacecraft began to tumble wildly and out of control. Armstrong immediately detached from the GATV, but the tumbling continued and then intensified. Gemini VIII was out of control.[40] An article in *Discovery* described the situation:

> "The men in Houston got confirmation that the spacecraft had separated just as Armstrong pulled the Gemini back and Scott hit the undock switch. Unfortunately, the separation didn't help the astronauts. Scott called down as calmly as he could, 'We have serious problems here. We're– we're tumbling end over end up here. We're disengaged from the Agena.' They tried to explain to mission control what was happening. 'We're rolling up and we can't turn anything off,' Armstrong said. 'Continuously increasing in a left roll.' Armstrong fought without success to dampen out the spacecraft's tumbling. Turning things over to Scott didn't help; he was equally unsuccessful. By then, Gemini 8 was making one full revolution *per second*. The centrifugal force building up inside the spacecraft was making loose items — flight plants, checklists, and procedure charts —

---

[38] "From the Mojave to the Moon: Neil Armstrong's Early NASA Years," http://www.nasa.gov/missions/research/neil_armstrong.html

[39] "Buzz Aldrin: Neil Armstrong Was the 'Best Pilot I Ever Knew," http://www.thedailybeast.com/articles/2012/08/27/buzz-aldrin-neil-armstrong-was-the-best-pilot-i-ever-knew.html;

[40] "Gemini 8," National Space Science: Data Center, http://nssdc.gsfc.nasa.gov/nmc/spacecraftDisplay.do?id=1966-020A;

stick to the walls. Their heads and arms were pinned against the backs of their seats making reaching the hand controllers an effort. The sunlight coming in through the windows was flashing as fast as a strobe light.[41]

**Gemini VIII**

The only thing Armstrong could do was end the flight and begin re-entry, since the alternative of Scott and him struck by a blackout would have doomed them. He reached back behind his seat and felt for the re-entry control system. Once engaged, the spacecraft stopped its tumble, and Scott fed line code into the computer to program new re-entry information. Gemini splashed down on Earth, and the investigation began. It turned out one of Gemini's eight control thrusters had been stuck in the on-position. When it fired thrust repeatedly, the spacecraft had responded by tumbling, but the crew of Gemini VIII had survived through their grasp of the situation and the creation of a solution to save the capsule. Armstrong's training as a pilot proved to be the most crucial factor. By avoiding a catastrophe, Armstrong had also kept NASA on track with its projected mission schedule for the Moon.[42]

[41] "The Vomit-inducing Gemini 8 Mission," http://news.discovery.com/space/history-of-space/neil-armstrong-at-the-helm-120730.htm

[42] "The Vomit-inducing Gemini 8 Mission," http://news.discovery.com/space/history-of-space/neil-armstrong-at-

## Chapter 4: Early Apollo Missions

Already by late 1961, NASA had begun to mention the "Lunar Excursion Module" (LEM) as the agency's choice to land men on the Moon. Events worked quickly to decide once and for all where the LEM would rendezvous with the other spacecraft, and when NASA confirmed the ascendance of LOR, the development of the LEM commenced in full. "Considerable analytical and experimental work was underway on engineering problems associated with landing the LEM on the Moon. Landing loads and stability were studied by dropping dynamically scaled models on simulated lunar soil and by computer runs which utilized mathematical models of both the LEM and the lunar surface. At the same time an effort was underway to deduce in engineering terms the surface characteristics and soil mechanics of the lunar surface, Only the sparse photographic information from Ranger [space probe] was available to the engineers, yet later data from Surveyor and Orbiter [space probes] led to no significant change in the LEM design."[43]

Apollo proceeded on pace, and what some would call a rushed pace; to keep pace with Gemini and maintain the ambitious schedule of goals, the Command Service Module (CSM) and LEM were sped along. The program meant for its maiden flight to carry three astronauts, quite a risk given the new technologies under use. But as each successive stage of the Saturn rocket shot into space, each uncrewed launch of mockups and different capsule mockups only put more pressure on the deadline to launch a manned Apollo flight. The authors of *The Apollo Spacecraft* explained, "While the Mercury and Gemini spacecraft were being developed and operated, the three-man Apollo program had grown in magnitude and complexity and included a command module, a service module, a lunar module, and a giant Saturn V rocket. The spacecraft and launch vehicle towered 110 meters above the launching pad, and weighed some 3 million kilograms. With the Apollo program, the missions and flight plans had become much more ambitious, the hardware had become more refined, the software had become more sophisticated, and ground support equipment also grew in proportion."[44]

If anything, too much success came too quickly. While Soviet space advances put pressure on NASA to speed up Apollo, the program's inflexible schedule created an inevitable moment of truth. The capsule that showed up at the Kennedy Space Center launch pad possessed more than 19 pounds of combustible materials, and the Apollo 1 mission ended tragically when a fire killed the three astronauts trapped board. When Apollo 204 Review Board's Final Report was published, it came up with two possible scenarios for the deaths of Gus Grissom, Ed White, and Roger Chafee. Frank Borman, Apollo astronaut, reported the findings of the investigatory committee on Apollo 1 tragedy: "We think that what happened, there was probably an electrical

---

the-helm-120730.htm

[43] *The Apollo Spacecraft - A Chronology*, Volume III, "Forward," Brooks, Courtney G. and Ivan D. Ertel, October 1, 1964 - January 20, 1966 (NASA SP-4009, 1973). http://www.hq.nasa.gov/office/pao/History/SP-4009/frwrd3.htm

[44] *The Apollo Spacecraft - A Chronology*, Volume III, "Forward," Newkirk, Roland W, Courtney G. Brooks, and Ivan D. Ertel, January 21, 1966 - July 13, 1974, (NASA SP-4009, 1978), http://www.hq.nasa.gov/office/pao/History/SP-4009/frwrd4.htm

short down at the lower equipment bay near Gus's left foot that created a spark. With 100 percent oxygen and a PSI of around twenty-one pounds, that spark propagated rapidly and became an explosion."[45]

**The crew of Apollo 1**

The struggle to build Apollo took its toll on the engineers and mechanics, and it ended with the abandonment of Launching pad 34 and a plaque: *Ad Astra per aspera...A rough path leads to the stars.* NASA went back to work on Apollo, knowing the Soviets would seize on the opportunity. Apollo 2 and 3 were cancelled, with their objectives segmented into other missions along with the Saturn V rocket.

Apollo 4, 5 and 6 were launched without crews; and when this was judged satisfactory, Apollo had its first flight crews. NASA could replace rockets, but it had a harder time to replace well-trained astronauts, the best pilots America possessed, even if they understood the "rough path" to the "stars" and heeded the words of Grissom: "If we die, we want people to accept it. We hope that is anything happens to us it will not delay the program. This conquest of space is worth the

---

[45] *Rocket Men*, 185.

risk of life."[46]

Still, the space program could ill afford to lose any more astronauts during training; and this is exactly what nearly occurred to Armstrong in his preparations for piloting the LEM. As early as 1960, NASA had planned for the proper simulator to train astronauts to land on the Moon, and after many ambitious proposals, NASA settled on the most complex of them all, the Lunar Landing Research Vehicle, a truss of lightweight aluminum mounted to a jet engine. There was a special mode called the lunar simulation mode that the pilot would engage, and the mode commanded the jet engine to support only five-sixths of the LLRV's weight. Along with this, it had a cockpit that rotated freely of the engine so the effect of lunar gravity could then be achieved. A pilot would sit in an open air cockpit, ascend like a plane, and then adjust the jets to behave as they would in lunar gravity. The pilot would then attempt to settle the craft down onto the ground, using the same controls of the LEM.

By 1968, Neil Armstrong and Pete Conrad were in line to command the first lunar missions. Their training took place at Dryden; and Armstrong and Conrad had made 20 and 13 flights respectively. For Armstrong's 21st test flight, the switch into lunar mode went off perfectly until the LLRV went sideways. Armstrong now flew the simulator on his side, and he attempted to right the trainer, but it failed to respond to his controls. The LLRV began to lose altitude rapidly, and Armstrong was left with little recourse but to eject. He did, floating away on a parachute just 200 feet off the ground as the LLRV crashed nearby and erupted into a fireball. Armstrong's only remark to his fellow astronauts was, "I had to bail out of the darn thing."[47] Five of the seven LLRVs ultimately crashed or blew up in flight, but no pilots died.

[46] *Rocket Men*, 190.
[47] "Apollo LLRV," Encyclopedia Astronautica, http://www.astronautix.com/craft/apoollrv.htm; "When Landing on the Moon, Practice Makes Perfect," http://news.discovery.com/space/history-of-space/when-landing-on-the-moon-practice-makes-perfect-120719.htm

**An LLRV**

What Armstrong took from that experience is worth mentioning because his skills, more than anything, justified his command of Apollo 11, and ultimately, his role as the first man to step on the Moon. Other factors have been considered for his choice as well: the military chain of command perspective, which favored Armstrong due to NASA's "naval genetic code"; an engineering perspective, with the LEM's design giving precedence to the command pilot who was closer to the door; and lastly, and the personality perspective, which most astronauts identified as Aldrin's "lack of finesse". But above all, Armstrong served as the logical choice due to the abilities he demonstrated as a pilot.[48] During test flights, he had demonstrated the best

---

[48] *Rocket Men*, 19.

qualities of an astronaut-engineer, one who could successfully lead a mission of the Apollo spacecraft and personally set foot on the lunar surface. Apollo was the epitome of technology and training, and Armstrong had all the characteristics of an individual best suited to command a mission from the Earth to the Moon, and most importantly, make the first manned landing.

The ambitiousness of the Saturn-Apollo schedule had cost it the lives of three astronauts, but with the resumption of the missions, NASA seemed back on track. However, the agency and the manned lunar program needed a significant morale boost that ambitions alone could not provide. While "Apollo Applications" provided a blueprint for the future -- lunar bases from used Saturn upper stages, LEM "trucks," and a Venus flyby mission -- the mid-1960s saw the U.S. and the Soviets in nearly the same position. Both seemed ready to launch missions to the Moon.

The U.S.S.R. had achieved a bunch of successes that gave America's space rival the ability to keep pace with the U.S. The soft-landing of the moon probe Luna 9 gave NASA great worry, as too did the rendezvous docking between Soyuz 1 and 2. With that, the Soviets appeared to have two important parts of a mission covered: lunar landing and orbital docking. Soon came the launching of Zond, a further modification of the Soyuz and a worthy rival to Apollo. The Zond was a spacecraft that, while in automated form, could theoretically make the trip to the Moon. The Soviets also stepped up their program with the launch of the LK Lunar Lander, and its impressive orbital maneuvers were later bookended by the other Soviet improvements to Soyuz, with another docking between missions 4 and 5. The Soviets had their moon craft and the ability to land. All they needed was a powerful enough booster, and one that was reliable.[49]

---

[49] "The Soviet Manned Lunar Program," ed. Marcus Lindroos, http://www.fas.org/spp/eprint/lindroos_moon1.htm; "LEK Lunar Expeditionary Complex," Encyclopedia Astronautica, http://astronautix.com/craft/lekmplex.htm; *Rocket Men*, 191, 195, 203.

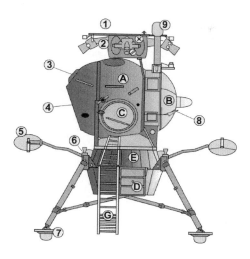

**The Soviet design**

The success of the Saturn-Apollo complex can be attributed to the original vision of NASA and the first professionals who guided the agency and its plans for spaceflight. More was needed than a reliable rocket; any lunar mission required the best computer and software to navigate and operate the spacecraft. The civilian contribution to U.S. spaceflight, despite its military leanings, began partly from a utopian vision for any type of "Space Race" between nations. Superpowers could compete with one another. As aerospace technologist Paul Lowman says of the success of Apollo, "It seems safe to suggest that his demonstration is a real contribution to prevention of a global thermonuclear war no potential aggressor could plan a surprise attack on the United States without taking into account the military strength implied by it."[50] In a sense, the Space Race kept the Cold War from heating up.

While the professionals who built, tested and launched the Saturn-Apollo complex of ships bore out the tough work of the engineering and mechanical corps of America, their dedication reflected the passion of one of manned spacecraft's founders: Wernher Von Braun, the expatriate rocket scientist from the defeated Third Reich. His military origin notwithstanding, von Braun was repeatedly stymied by U.S. military leaders, even though he did actively court them by touting the benefits of manned spaceflight. Rejected, he offered his vision to the American public, who eagerly read his vision in *Collier's* magazine as early as 1952. With visions of winged rockets and space stations in the public's head, von Braun found it easy to outline a "new" Manhattan Project, one that NASA would eventually adopt, and a blueprint that NASA

---

[50] *Rocket Men*, 91.

would use to court the public sector. No other place demonstrated this early collaboration of civilian and military rocket scientists than Huntsville, Alabama, known also as "Rocket City." Here the first non-military rocket professionals worked on the first rockets to carry Americans into outer space, and a government-funded and civilian-led space program began.[51]

NASA's use of civilian contractors hired by the government created an initial problem that was never properly fixed by the time of Apollo. The agency never had enough experience, which meant that any astronauts who strapped themselves into a capsule on top of a Saturn rocket were in the hands of professionals who were forced to invent spacecraft systems. Despite the gap in experience, the civilian engineers responded with specific knowledge in unproven fields, most notably their invention of escape systems for astronauts in the event of a launch pad accident.[52] After Apollo 1, Nelson explained, "Pad catastrophe was such a grave responsibility, in fact, that NASA had engineered a number of methods to rescue its crews. The key system was a three rocket apparatus -- the launch escape tower -- attached to *Columbia's* [Apollo 11's SC] nose cone, ready to fire, pull the men from their booster, deploy the chutes, and drift into an Atlantic splashdown.[53]

While the engineers and technicians found themselves in tight situations to design launch systems, the Apollo astronauts themselves found themselves increasingly stressed by the pervasive doubts about the quality and duration of their training. "Apollo 11's Neil Armstrong, Buzz Aldrin, and Michael Collins did not themselves feel adequately trained. But they were afraid to admit this to [Deke] Slayton [flight crew operations director]. 'Neil used to come home with his face drawn white, and I was worried about him,' Armstrong's wife, Jan, remembered. 'I was worried about all of them. The worst period was in early June. Their morale was down. They were worried about whether there was time enough for them to learn the things they had to learn, to do the things they had to do, if this mission was to work.'[54]

At the same time, NASA had to deal with requesting funding from a Congress that remembered the early rocket disasters and responded to the space agency's request for money with a modest budget to fund the Saturn rocket. The perception of the civilians who worked on Saturn and Apollo was that their own government prevented them from the creation of an adequate program that could challenge the Soviets and beat them to the Moon.[55] Ultimately, computers made a significant difference in the Apollo Program's success by boosting American confidence in the ability of astronauts to pilot a craft to orbit, land, and return from the Moon. The *Columbia* command module possessed two 17.5-pound Raytheon computers, and the lunar module *Eagle* had one computer. The memory of each one was 36K. While far less impressive

---

[51] Rocket Men, 109, 112.

[52] *Rocket Men*, 145.

[53] *Rocket Men*, 7.

[54] *Rocket Men*, 13.

[55] *Rocket Men*, 150.

than early 21ˢᵗ century cell phones, each computer was much more spectacular in its function, and especially its importance. Nothing was more vital to a mission to the Moon than the computer system with the responsibility to chart the course and deliver the spacecraft to the intended target. This was Guidance and Navigation, which was tasked with guiding the Apollo spacecraft across 250,000 miles of space, orbit around the Moon, land at a targeted location on the surface, guide the *Eagle* from the surface back to the *Columbia* in orbit, guide the *Columbia* towards a space in the Earth's atmosphere that would "capture" the capsule; and land the *Columbia* near a recovery ship in the Pacific Ocean. As Nelson put it in *Rocket Men*, "G&N consisted of a miniature computer with an incredible amount of information in its memory; an array of gyroscopes and accelerometers called the inertial-measurement unit; and a space sextant to enable the navigator to make star sightings. Together they determined precisely the spacecraft location between Earth and Moon, and how best to burn the engines to correct the ship's course or to land at the right spot on the Moon with a minimum expenditure of fuel."[56]

Computers were, in many regards, the key to Apollo 11 solving the key problem of the mission: a circular lunar orbit needed for insertion. How well the astronauts worked with the G&N would leave them with a decision on the far side of the Moon. Either they could use the systems to correct their path to enter orbit, or they would have to burn engines to abort the mission and return home.[57] At least in that scenario, the lives of the astronauts would be saved by the computers, while the tough decision to land or not would be avoided by the cool calculation of a computer.

[56] *Rocket Men*, 220-221.
[57] *Rocket Men*, 225.

**The display and keyboard of the Apollo Guidance Computer on the *Columbia***

The helpful advice of a computer might not always be heeded though. During computer simulations of a mission, Armstrong and ground control repeatedly had heated discussions over the possibility of abort, especially if Earth-based radar perceived a threat to landing. In this case, Armstrong refused to defer to computers and rely on his own intuition, which worried NASA mission controllers. They were fearful that a pilot like Armstrong would decide to make a decision that computer simulations said he could not survive, and further ignore the advice of the computers in Houston.[58] NASA was so worried about the possibilities that President Nixon prepared a speech for the event of Apollo 11's crash or inability to leave the Moon.[59] Nixon's statement read:

> "Fate has ordained that the men who went to the moon to explore in peace will stay on the moon to rest in peace. These brave men, Neil Armstrong and Edwin Aldrin, know that there is no hope for their recovery. But they also know that

---

[58] *Rocket Men*, 65.
[59] *Rocket Men*, 69.

there is hope for mankind in their sacrifice. These two men are laying down their lives in mankind's most noble goal: the search for truth and understanding. They will be mourned by their families and friends; they will be mourned by their nation; they will be mourned by the people of the world; they will be mourned by a Mother Earth that dared send two of her sons into the unknown. In their exploration, they stirred the people of the world to feel as one; in their sacrifice, they bind more tightly the brotherhood of man. In ancient days, men looked at stars and saw their heroes in the constellations. In modern times, we do much the same, but our heroes are epic men of flesh and blood. Others will follow and surely find their way home. Man's search will not be denied. But these men were the first, and they will remain the foremost in our hearts. For every human being who looks up at the moon in the nights to come will know that there is some corner of another world that is forever mankind."[60]

## Chapter 5: Finishing Touches

A great deal of anxiety surrounded NASA about the quality of the rockets and spaceships, the training of the ground crews and astronauts, and the coordination between humans and computers. For Apollo, disaster was much closer to reality than anyone wanted to admit. Already, tragedy had struck the program during Apollo 1.

Two things happened that put Apollo on course to land on the Moon. The first was Apollo 8, the first all-up mission of a Saturn V and a crewed ship towards the Moon. Understandably, most people can name Apollo 11 as the first mission to land men on the Moon, and a critically acclaimed film about Apollo 13's harrowing mission was released in 1995, but this has also meant that the rest of the Apollo missions have been greatly overshadowed, including Apollo 8, despite the fact Apollo 8 accomplished several firsts and ultimately made Apollo 11 possible.

NASA launched Apollo 7 on October 11, 1968. Apollo 7 was a manned mission that tested the command/service modules in Earth's orbit and reentry. The successful mission demonstrated the viability of the command/service module to enter Earth's orbit and survive reentry back into the Earth's atmosphere. Apollo 8 was originally intended to test the lunar module in orbit and reentry, as Apollo 7 had done for the command/service module, but in June 1968, NASA suffered a setback with the lunar modules, which compromised the planned December 1968 date for Apollo 8's launch.

Since the lunar modules weren't ready, and the command/service modules had already been successfully tested in Earth's orbit and reentry, NASA decided in August to change Apollo 8's mission, making it a manned mission to orbit around the Moon in the command/service module.

---

[60] "Read the Speech Nixon Prepared in Case the Apollo 11 Astronauts Died on the Moon," http://io9.com/5880226/read-the-speech-nixon-prepared-in-case-the-apollo-11-astronauts-died-on-the-moon

This would allow NASA to test the command/service module's lunar orbit procedures, and, of course, score a huge propaganda victory in the Space Race.

On December 21, 1968, Apollo 8 was launched by a Saturn V rocket. All three stages of the Saturn V rocket had been tested in previous launches, including the crucial third stage that had to reactivate to accelerate the spacecraft out of Earth's orbit and toward the Moon. The previous unmanned mission suffered a failure of the third stage's Trans Lunar Injection sequence, but the Saturn V carrying Apollo 8 worked almost perfectly. About three hours after launching, the Apollo 8 crew became the first humans to escape Earth's orbit and take pictures of the entire planet as a whole.

Apollo 8 cruised toward the Moon for nearly three whole days before it was time for the Lunar Orbit Insertion. Four minutes later, the crew became the first humans to enter the Moon's orbit and see the far side of the Moon in person. While orbiting, the crew reconnoitered the Moon's surface, eventually describing the "Sea of Tranquility" well enough that it would become Apollo 11's planned landing site.

As Apollo 8 continued orbiting around the Moon, it witnessed the Earth rising and snapped the iconic "Earthrise" photo of the globe from the Moon's vantage point on December 24. On Christmas Day, after several orbits around the Moon and the first ever live broadcast interview from the Moon's orbit, Apollo 8 prepared to head home.

On the voyage home, crewmember Jim Lovell inadvertently switched off certain navigational readings for the module's computers. This accident required using the module's thrusters to manually realign the spacecraft for reentry. The mistake was quickly corrected, but it fortuitously gave Lovell the experience to do it for Apollo 13 under more trying circumstances.

On the afternoon of December 27, 1968, Apollo 8 splashed down safely in the Pacific Ocean. In addition to setting history, the three crewmembers, Lovell, Frank Borman and William Anders, were named Time's Men of the Year.

The success of a mission that orbited the Moon and returned home reinvigorated NASA and the Apollo Program. The success of the mission proved what many at NASA had said for a year. Saturn could launch men to the Moon; and the Soviets and their N-1 booster -- it continued to explode on the launch pad or fall back to the Earth. It seemed the U.S. had the space it needed to beat the Soviets.[61] All that was left was to launch and pilot Apollo 11.

---

[61] *Rocket Men*, 195.

**Picture of Earth taken by Apollo 8**

Apollo 8's success had also benefited its backup crew, which included Neil Armstrong and Buzz Aldrin. Neil Armstrong later explained:

> "We were very excited about [Apollo 8]...We thought it was very bold, because we still had the problem on the Saturn and we'd had a couple problems with [both] Saturn V launches, so to take the next one, and without those problems being demonstrated as solved, and put men, a crew on it, not just take it into orbit, to take it to the Moon, it seemed incredibly aggressive. But we were for it. We thought that was a wonderful opportunity. If we could make it work, why, it would make us a giant leap ahead. It showed a lot of courage on the part of NASA

management to make that step. One of the things I was concerned with at the time was whether our navigation was sufficiently accurate, that we could, in fact, devise a trajectory that would get us around the Moon at the right distance without, say, hitting the Moon on the back side of something like that, and if we lost communication with Earth, for whatever reason, could we navigate by ourselves using celestial navigation. We thought we could, but these were undemonstrated skills."[62]

The Gemini program prepared to conclude its original mission objective as a trainer of Apollo astronauts in the year 1966, and the 10th mission rocketed into space carrying astronauts Michael Collins and John W. Young. They had a full mission in front of them, charged with the accomplishment of former Gemini objectives left unfulfilled by the cancellation of missions. Collins and Young's flight had big ramifications that made Apollo 8 successful, including the ability to dock with an Agena module, fire the module's rockets, achieve a higher orbit to rendezvous with another Agena module (one that was derelict and without radar) and perform a space walk over to the module. Every step that Gemini X achieved gave NASA the confidence that Apollo 8's lunar flyby could be completed. So successful was Gemini X that NASA would give Collins the responsibility as the command/service module (CSM) pilot on Apollo 8.

---

[62] *Rocket Men*, 198.

**Michael Collins**

An emergency back surgery took Collins off the mission and nearly ended his astronaut career, but his recovery allowed NASA to put him back won the Apollo Program and on the next available mission for the Moon. With Apollo 10's successful mock-up and rehearsal for the Moon landing in lunar orbit, NASA could put Collins in the pilot seat of the CSM *Columbia* on Apollo 11.[63]

Michael Collins (b. October 31, 1930) was a rarity among NASA astronauts. He was a United States Air Forces test pilot, far different than the greater pool of pilots NASA recruited from, which typically included aviators from the Navy and Marine Corps. His 5,000 hours spent in the air gave him excellent control of the "stick," which led to his inclusion in the Astronaut Group Three of 1963 and made him one of the best pilots in NASA.[64] He was used to carrying out experimental missions and was perfectly comfortable in that capacity. He would be required to

[63] "Gemini X (10)," http://nssdc.gsfc.nasa.gov/nmc/masterCatalog.do?sc=1966-066A

[64] "Biographical Data (Michael Collins)," http://www.jsc.nasa.gov/Bios/htmlbios/collins-m.html; "Astronaut Group Three," http://grin.hq.nasa.gov/ABSTRACTS/GPN-2000-001476.html

accomplish pilot-tasks that no other aviator had ever done, primarily the one thing no Apollo mission could test for: the rendezvous with a lunar module on-return from the Moon with two astronauts onboard. Years later Collins remarked on the test of his skills as an aviator he would most likely be remembered for: "My secret terror for the last six months has been leaving them on the Moon and returning to Earth alone; now I am within minutes of finding out the truth of the matter...If they fail to rise from the surface, or crash back into it, I am not going to commit suicide; I am coming home, forthwith, but I will be a marked man for life and I know it."[65]

A good solution for Collins to avoid the infamy of "stranding" Armstrong and Aldrin on the Moon lay with the Guidance and Navigation system. Computers and navigation software were one part of it, and gyroscopes also helped a pilot keep track of the three-dimensions of outer space; but it was the experience of Collins that made the difference in the success of Apollo. Collins, like the Apollo astronauts before and after him, would wear an eye patch to avoid the fatigue of endless hours of squinting. He peered through the ship's sextant to sight stars in the night sky, no different than navigators had done for hundreds of generations on board sailing ships. When he located the position and altitudes of the stars, he combined the results with the onboard data of the ship's speed and position. The purpose of this was to fire the CSM's rocket and send Apollo 11 on its course to the Moon.[66]

The Guidance and Navigation unit was only as good as its human operator, and that responsibility also lay with Collins. When the gyroscopes were correctly set, Collins was in charge with the dial-in of the position of the two reference stars. The navigation system would then compare the ship's position with the Inertial Measuring Unit, and the thrusters were fired to set the ship on its course. The problem with this, as Apollo 8, 9, and 10 learned, was that the amount of sunlight hitting the spacecraft made it difficult to recognize stars without the surrounding constellations. Collins proved good at using the sextant's computer to find the stars.[67]

Collins' proficiency with the challenges of flight and navigation worked to ease the many problems Apollo faced in landing men on the Moon. For one, serious gaps in knowledge about the Moon's composition challenged NASA, and that serious lack of data could potentially compromise the mission. The Ranger and Surveyor probes had done an excellent job mapping the Moon, but the astronauts had a feeling that, along with their training, there was not enough knowledge of the surface terrain to inform targeted landing sites.[68]

Collins also worried about things out of his control, mainly the technologies that were responsible for landing the LEM *Eagle* on the Moon and the return trip. The LEM's upper stage,

[65] "How Michael Collins Became the Forgotten Astronaut of Apollo 11," http://www.guardian.co.uk/science/2009/jul/19/michael-collins-astronaut-apollo11
[66] *Rocket Men*, 220.
[67] *Rocket Men*, 221.
[68] *Rocket Men*, 230.

the vehicle responsible for the delivery of Armstrong and Aldrin from the Moon's surface to the CSM in orbit, had developed an instability. Sometimes during dress-rehearsals, it would not separate from the descent stage. This would have trapped the astronauts on the Moon.[69]

Another issue that developed belonged to the contingencies of things the engineers at NASA could not plan for and would only know at the moment of truth, when the *Eagle* was on its way to the lunar surface. Engineers questioned whether imaging radar would work on the LEM, and whether or not the data could be simultaneously communicated with the CSM and Mission Control back on Earth.[70] The matter of docking the *Columbia* and *Eagle* also gave NASA fits, as the history of near disasters during rendezvous and space walks had never been completely solved. Most astronauts had gotten sick during EVAs outside of their spaceship, as the strain to maneuver in zero gravity fatigued them. NASA knew in an emergency that EVAs might be all that could save the crew, especially if Armstrong and Aldrin had to move from the LEM to the CSM.[71]

NASA flight managers and Apollo astronauts, aware of all the things that could go wrong, counted on the skill and dedication of professionals like Collins to offset the challenges and dangers that could potentially destroy the mission. His position as the CSM pilot carried a great honor and responsibility. No astronaut could pilot the capsule unless they had done before. At that time in the flight order of Apollo astronauts, none had, so Collins was the only astronaut who NASA felt could be entrusted with the job to circle the Moon alone and await the two astronauts who would descend to the surface and hopefully return. As Armstrong put it:

"I was certainly aware that this was a culmination of the work of 300,000 or 400,000 people over a decade and that the nation's hopes and outward appearance largely rested on how the results came out...And you know, I have no complaints about the way my colleagues were able to step up to that....when you have hundreds of thousands of people all doing their job a little better than they have to, you get an improvement in performance. And that's the reason we could have pulled this whole thing off...when I was working here at the Manned Spacecraft Center, you could stand across the street and you could not tell when quitting time was, because people didn't leave at quitting time in those days. People just worked, and they worked until whatever their job was [was] done...And whenever you have those ingredients, whether it be government or private industry or a retail store, you're going to win."[72]

[69] *Rocket Men*, 12.
[70] *Rocket Men*, 17.
[71] *Rocket Men*, 297.
[72] *Rocket Men*, 81-82.

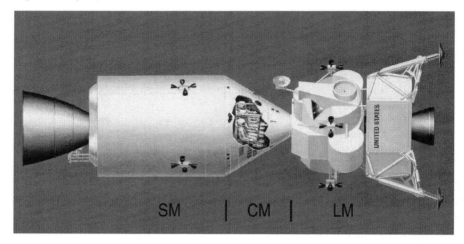

**The service module, command module, and lunar module design for Apollo 11**

At the end of 1968, the country was celebrating the historic and successful Apollo 8 mission, as was NASA. But NASA also realized that the mission only occurred due to a setback with the lunar module that would actually land on the Moon. In March 1969, the unheralded Apollo 9 tested the lunar module's maneuvers for several days in Earth's orbit before successfully reentering Earth's atmosphere.

By May 1969, NASA was ready to do an entire dry run of landing men on the Moon. Apollo 10 was sent into lunar orbit with the command/service module and lunar module, and on May 22, a lunar module descended toward the Moon for the first time. The lunar module was manned, but the ascent stage was not fully fueled, so it could not complete an entire descent. The automated system worked, and the modules successfully re-docked together. Apollo 10 successfully splashed down on May 26, and with that, NASA was ready to land men on the Moon.

Before Collins could pilot the CSM with attached LEM to the Moon, the Saturn V booster needed to accomplish the most dangerous part of the mission: the launch. The astronauts rode the high-speed elevator 320 feet to the Apollo capsule and strapped into their flight seats. The countdown began at 2 hours and 46 minutes. The Soviets struggled throughout the 1960s to design rockets up to the task, but NASA got it right with the Saturn V rocket, which to this day remains the most powerful launching rocket NASA ever used. The Saturn V rockets were truly gargantuan, standing nearly 350 feet tall and holding thousands of tons of fuel. These rockets could carry a payload weighing over 250,000 pounds into orbit, giving it the ability to launch the

Apollo spacecraft into orbit in about 12 minutes at nearly 18,000 miles per hour. But that was just the beginning of the Saturn V's duties. Once in orbit, the Saturn V still had to accelerate the spacecraft to nearly 25,000 miles per hour to allow the spacecraft to escape the Earth's orbit and head for the Moon.

Designing rocket engines that powerful was hard enough, but NASA had to design the Saturn V to accomplish its duties in multiple stages, because an Apollo spacecraft typically had to spend a few hours in orbit around the Earth before heading for the Moon. Thus, the Saturn V's first two stages would accelerate the spacecraft to about 15,000 miles per hour, while the third and final stage would enter the spacecraft into Earth's orbit at about 18,000 miles per hour. But this third and final stage also had to be capable of essentially restarting and reaccelerating to propel the spacecraft out of Earth's orbit and to the Moon at about 25,000 miles per hour. Not only was Saturn V capable of getting the job done, but it also got the job done successfully every time it was used. NASA relied on Saturn V rockets more than a dozen times without a major accident during the 1960s and 1970s.

With the last adjustments made to leaky hydrogen fuel valves, the five mammoth F-1 engines fired. The rocket lifted, moving slightly -- some astronauts called it a faint 'wobble' -- and the rockets gimbaled slightly to keep everything on course. Nothing held the spaceship upright but the columns of thrust. A launch controller said the words the crew most wanted to hear: the rocket had cleared the tower. Within seconds, Apollo 11 was lifted hundreds of feet into the air and its auto program began a roll. The ship was on course towards the first objective. The first stage of the Saturn V rocket would accelerate the spacecraft to over 6,000 miles per hour in two and a half minutes before detaching and falling away. The second stage accelerated the spacecraft to about 15,000 miles per hour after six more minutes before falling away. If all went well, Apollo 11 would orbit the Earth in a little more than 11 minutes.[73]

---

[73] "Apollo Flight Journey," Apollo 11, Day 1, Part 1: Launch, http://www.hq.nasa.gov/alsj/a11/a11.html

**The Launch Control Center before liftoff**

After two orbits of the Earth, Collins was commanded by Houston Control to ignite the third stage of the Saturn V, known as the "Translunar Injection". This stage would accelerate the spacecraft to about 25,000 mph to reach the escape velocity necessary to escape Earth's orbit. At this time, the lunar module attached to the service/command module, and once the spacecraft reached escape velocity, the Saturn V's third stage fell away on a different trajectory.

**Apollo 11's picture of Earth during the Translunar Injection**

The engines fired on and shot Apollo 11 on its course to the Moon, a journey that would take three days of cruising and a short engine burst known as the "Lunar Orbit Insertion" procedure to properly position the spacecraft to be captured by the Moon's orbit. NASA had mapped the Moon during previous missions, in order to help choose the landing sites for the Apollo lunar modules. When the Moon captured the spacecraft, the spacecraft would complete several orbits around the Moon to properly line up the lunar module for descent.

### Chapter 7: Traveling to the Moon

As this part of the journey began, Aldrin turned on the color camera inside the capsule, and already viewers on Earth witnessed the historic trip that might or might not land men on the Moon. Of course, one thing the camera could not capture was the mental state inside the capsule. Nelson captured the mood in *Rocket Men* by describing how Collins felt about the other two astronauts:

> "Of the three, Collins was always the 'easy-going guy who brought levity into things,' as Buzz Aldrin recalled. During the run-up to their mission, Collins tried to foster a sense of camaraderie, but could only get so far. After Armstrong's bulwark of shyness proved impenetrable, Collins decided that Neil 'never transmits anything but the surface layer, and that only sparingly. I like him, but I don't know what to make of him, or how to get to know him better.' He doesn't seem willing to meet you halfway...Buzz, on the other hand, is more approachable; in fact, for reasons I cannot fully explain, it is me that seems to be trying to keep him at arm's length. I have the feeling that he would probe me for weaknesses, and that makes me uncomfortable."[74]

Perhaps the astronauts, much to the chagrin of the "easy-going" Collins, were men much more comfortable with their thoughts. The view of the Earth from orbit had already inspired the crew and left them to ponder the "imaginary lines that you can't see."[75] Once on the way to the Moon, though, having left the Earth behind, no reference points existed. Only the blackness of space awaited them; and the spaceship was engulfed by the expanse of dark and the glitter of stars.[76]

All the crew could do at this point was go through their various duties; Collins attended to the tasks of purging fuel cells, dumping wastewater, recharging batteries, and replacing carbon dioxide filters. Armstrong and Aldrin went over procedures to land. They also had to eat. "On Apollo 11, ham, tuna, and chicken salad sandwich spreads were squeezed out of a tube...Freeze dried entrees...of roast beef, ham, potatoes, yam, bacon, applesauce, vegetable medley, and hash were vacuum-sealed in plastic and needed to be rehydrated with three shots of hot water and kneaded into a mush, which was then, again, squeezed out like toothpaste."[77]

Still, the astronauts on Apollo 11 enjoyed the trip, especially the sensation of weightlessness,[78] and Apollo 11 experienced a unique visual phenomenon on the way to the Moon. The further the ship traveled, the harder it became to see the Moon. Collins pitched the ship so the crew could have a view of their destination, but they did not have much time to appreciate the view. On July 19, the fourth day of the mission, they would make the burn of the CSM's single thruster to achieve orbit. This, like other events on the trip, was the moment of truth. Either Apollo 11 would successfully enter the orbit of the Moon in order to land on the surface, or the burn would

---

[74] *Rocket Men*, 43.

[75] *Rocket Men*, 212.

[76] *Rocket Men*, 216.

[77] *Rocket Men*, 217.

[78] *Rocket Men*, 218.

fail and they would have to abort the mission.

NASA soon received the signal from the dark side of the Moon, where Apollo 11 had now entered. They were "go" for lunar orbit. The mission to land on the Moon was still on.[79]

Looking out over the lunar surface, the crew lauded the near-perfect precision of the orbital insertion and compared notes about their perceptions of the Moon's "true" color. NASA asked them to identify the "landing path," and the crew looked for identifying craters, with a sudden panic at the realization that the topography nearly looked identical from one section to the other. Collins and Armstrong eventually made headway of the location of their bearings, but they quickly realized the Moon's true mystery. To the astronauts, the Moon was an "unwelcoming" and "unfriendly" place.[80] Collins later reflected on that moment, "I feel that all of us are aware that the honeymoon is over and we are about to lay our little pink bodies on the line...We have not been able to see the Moon for nearly a day now, and the change is electrifying....The Moon changes character as the angle of sunlight strikes its surface changes....It starts off very forbidding, becomes friendly and then becomes forbidding again as the Sun disappears."[81]

Indeed, Collins was right. The moment came to put their "little pink bodies on the line." After 13 orbits around the Moon, Armstrong and Aldrin dressed in the EVA suits, also known as "white, thirteen-layered, Mylar-and-Teflon-coated beta-cloth Integrated Thermal Meteoroid Garments."[82] Both astronauts took their positions inside the LEM *Eagle*. Collins also had to dress-up in a spacesuit, just in case he needed to make an emergency spacewalk.

To descend thousands of feet down to the Moon's surface, the lunar module had both an engine and thrusters that would allow it to maintain speed, control and direction. The lunar module would descend in a pirouette to help it descend straight, but as Apollo 11's lunar module inadvertently proved, any incorrect timing or ill-timed thrust would land a module several miles away from its intended destination, which could be the difference between a smooth landing or landing among boulders and craters. For most of the descent, the lunar module was automated, but the final stage of the descent required manual controls, and once the descent stage was finished, it would fall away from the module like the Saturn V rocket stages.

[79] *Rocket Men*, 226.
[80] *Rocket Men*, 226.
[81] *Rocket Men*, 227.
[82] *Rocket Men*, 233.

Armstrong and Aldrin did not sit down in the cockpit; they would fly the *Eagle* in an upright position, velcroed and tethered to the walls and floors. The LEM's appearance was function over form, appearing almost like an insect. It had the thinnest of skins, consisting of barely three sheets of aluminum foil. As one engineer explained, "aesthetics be hanged." The bug-eyed lander would accomplish the final vision of NASA's moon mission and land two men on the Moon by operating like a dinghy. The lower descent engine and stage would be left on the surface, and the ascent stage would bring the astronauts back to the *Columbia*, only to be cut loose and left to drift away into space.[83]

### Chapter 8: One Small Step for Man

Once Collins blew the explosive bolts, the *Eagle* now operated under its own electrical power. Armstrong swiveled the LEM around, so Collins could check the full deployment of its landing legs. Armstrong, as mission commander, gave the signal, "The Eagle has wings."

---

[83] *Rocket Men*, 234.

Now came the moment no amount of simulation could have anticipated, and the moment NASA and the astronauts feared most of all. No matter the amount of training, fine tunings in orbital calculation and speed were still not as exact as mission planners would have liked. And sure enough, the first problem of the many still to come occurred when the separation between *Columbia* and *Eagle* created more thrust than intended. Along with the mistakes in calculating the gravity of the Moon and its influence on the ships, this ensured the original landing site would be overshot by four miles, setting the *Eagle* on a path towards a field of boulders.[84]

Back on Earth in Houston at Mission Control (MOCR), a sprawling community college-like campus, the situation was closely monitored by an imaginative and dedicated corps of controllers who prided themselves on their ability to solve problems. They now would have one. In front of the 20x10 foot screen showing the two tiny dots that were *Columbia* and *Eagle* flashing slowly across a giant picture of the Moon, the controllers sat in a place nicknamed the Trench. Each one's role was designated by terms like "FLIGHT," "CONTROL," "FIDO," "TELMU," and "GUIDO." Flight dynamics officers, guidance and navigators imagined themselves as pilots on the spacecraft, in an effort to be so involved in their responsibilities that they literally connected with each phase of the mission.[85]

However, none of them realized that the *Eagle* would overshoot its landing target, because they were too wrapped up in another dilemma: Mission Control had lost radio contact with the *Eagle*. The controls then made a succession of confirmations, whether the *Eagle* could continue its powered descent and land, or whether or not to abort the mission. Given the choice of "Go/No Go," the responses were unanimous. A solution to the problem had lay with using Collins in the CSM to relay Mission Control telemetry to the LEM. The mission could continue. The flight controllers were all "Go." Collins relayed the message to the *Eagle*, "*Eagle, Columbia*. They just gave you a go for powered descent...*Eagle*, do you read *Columbia*?" Aldrin sent back the response, "We read you."[86]

Aldrin called off the instrument readings for Armstrong to pilot the craft, who by this time already realized they would overshoot the target area by almost four miles. MOCR realized the issue too as the *Eagle* sped over the surface of the Moon much faster than anticipated. MOCR considered aborting but waved it off. The controller responded with "GOs", and MOCR then lost contact with the LEM again.[87]

Making matters worse, computer alarms began to sound off. First came "Error 1202." MOCR learned of the programming error, knowing a computer malfunction would stop the mission, and both Apollo astronauts and flight controllers had trained for these alarms. In simulations, they

[84] *Rocket Men*, 236.
[85] *Rocket Men*, 240.
[86] *Rocket Men*, 245-246
[87] *Rocket Men*, 247.

had faced every single imaginable situation that could go wrong with the computers, and what they had learned instructed them for their next decision: "Go/No Go". As MOCR conferred with each other, Aldrin and Armstrong continued to descend rapidly to the Moon's surface.[88] Aldrin would later state, "During the descent, when were started having problems with the computer, my attention was focused entirely inside the cockpit looking at the displays and trying to relay the information on the computer and also on the altitude and altitude rate meters to Neil so he could use this with his out-the-window determination as to where we should go to find a suitable landing place. Things were happening fairly fast and it was just a question of making sure the most correct thing was done from my standpoint at that instance. Not much time was allowed for reflection on the situation."[89]

Then another error alarm sounded, "1201." Guidance and Navigation in MOCR reflected on the simulations training sessions for what seemed to Armstrong to be an unbearable amount of time. He asked for a reading, concerned that the powered descent could not continue. Armstrong later explained, "The concern here was not with the landing area we were going into, but, rather, whether we could continue at all. Consequently, our attention was directed toward clearing the program alarms, keeping the machine flying, and assuring ourselves that control was adequate to continue without requiring an abort. Most of the attention was directed inside the cockpit during this time period and, in my view, this would account for our inability to study the landing site and final landing location during the final descent. It wasn't until we got below two thousand feet that we were actually able to look out and view the landing area."

After 15 minutes of deciding, MOCR finally concluded that the computer alarm signaled the computer's difficulty with complex commands. The guidance system was being flooded by too many commands, and MOCR reassured *Eagle* that it could continue the descent. Armstrong still had control, and MOCR gave him another round of "GOs." Powered descent continued.

Armstrong tilted the *Eagle* into the feet-first position to land and immediately realized the terrain did not offer a place to safely land. They flew over a crater field with boulders, some the size of cars, so Armstrong continued to fly the *Eagle* horizontally. MOCR noticed his speed and the time; in every simulated landing, and by intended design, Armstrong should have landed the *Eagle* by now. Moreover, the craft was intended to land automatically. It had not, because Armstrong could not chance the site below him, so he continued to manually control the *Eagle* and skim over the top of the boulder field about 200 feet off the ground.

Armstrong had a number of other things to consider. A message light signaled a thruster shutdown, but he knew from the hundreds of flight simulations this was not the case, and because he knew that, he could continue to land. Fuel was a bigger concern. He now needed to rapidly lower the *Eagle* to the ground. At 65 feet, the LEM had 60 seconds of fuel left. With the

---

[88] "Apollo 11 Crew Makes Ready," http://www.hq.nasa.gov/pao/History/SP-4214/ch9-4.html#source23
[89] *Rocket Men*, 248.

rate of speed Armstrong had commanded the *Eagle* to move at, the craft entered the "dead-zone" quicker than MOCR liked. Even if Armstrong did decide to abort, the ascent stage would not lift them off in time to stop their descent to the surface. They would crash with fuel or without it.

These events happened without any explanation from Armstrong, so no one in the MOCR knew why he had decided to take manual control. He never said anything, and the flight controllers only heard Aldrin call off the feet and the percent of remaining fuel: "Four forward. Four forward. Drifting to the right a little...Twenty feet, down a half...Drifting forward just a little bit; that's good..."[90]

When Armstrong saw a clearing, he began to land, and the descent engines kicked up a cloud of dust. One of the *Eagle's* foot sensors had made contact. Armstrong heard Aldrin call "contact" and shut down the engines before relaying a famous message: "Houston, Tranquility Base here. The *Eagle* has landed."[91]

Small disconnects typified the momentous moment of triumph. A world celebrated, NASA

---

[90] *Rocket Men*, 258.
[91] *Rocket Men*, 259.

fretted, Aldrin turned to his religion, and Armstrong prepared to walk out onto an alien world. While people all over the world celebrated the *Eagle's* touchdown, MOCR had to make a decision: "Stay/No Stay." Another problem developed immediately upon landing when a frozen dollop of propellant blocked the descent stage engine and produced an increase in temperature. Engineers feared an explosion of the fuel vapors, but the problem solved itself, allowing Armstrong and Aldrin to resume their checklists. They would soon exit the *Eagle* and walk on the Moon's surface, but first, Aldrin took out his personal belongings and prepared to take Holy Communion.[92]

**Walter Cronkite holding up the *New York Times* headline**

Once the Eagle landed, the plan was to have Armstrong and Aldrin spend a few hours completely shutting down the lunar module and then get some sleep. But Aldrin and Armstrong were too excited to sleep. Armstrong prepared for several tasks before he would step out onto the Moon, and it took him and Aldrin far longer than expected -- 3 hours -- to suit up in spacesuits that would protect them. Armstrong also had to deploy the boom arm with another unique responsibility; the boom possessed a video camera to transmit the images of his first step onto the Moon. Armstrong, used to problems at this stage, also had to step a full three-and-a-half feet to the surface, but his landing was so gentle that the shock absorbers did not compress.[93]

---

[92] *Rocket Men*, 266.
[93] "Ten Things You Didn't Know about the Apollo 11 Moon Landing," http://www.popsci.com/military-aviation-amp-space/article/2009-06/40-years-later-ten-things-you-didnt-know-about-apollo-ii-moon-landing

**The picture of Armstrong taken by the camera on the boom**

Just before 11:00 p.m. Eastern Daylight Time, Armstrong began his exit out of the *Eagle* and onto the Moon's surface. As Armstrong was departing the *Eagle*, he activated the television camera, beginning a broadcast watched live by hundreds of millions of people. As he left his first footprint on the surface and described the dust, Armstrong then began to give his prepared statement, "That's one small step for a man, one giant leap for mankind."

Ever since, historians have debated whether Armstrong actually tripped over the statement, because the transmission sounded like he said, "That's one small step for man." The transmission quality of the video and audio was less than optimal, and some believe that a cut-out in sound produced what most people heard: "That's one small step for...man, one giant leap for mankind." Theories continue to abound about the omission of one "a" in the statement. Whether it was the transmission quality, nerves, or how a "central Ohioan" talks is a matter that might forever be unsettled. But the debate about the missing "a" demonstrated how many people on the Earth witnessed his first steps onto the Moon.[94]

---

[94] "One small step for 'a'...and a machine," http://www.collectspace.com/news/news-100306a.html; "Neil

Once he had made his first step, Armstrong let MOCR know what the surface was like, transmitting the message, "Yes, the surface is fine and powdery. I can kick it up loosely with my toe. It does adhere in fine layers, like powdered charcoal, to the sole and sides of my boots. I only go in a small fraction of an inch, maybe an eighth of an inch, but I can see the footprints of my boots and the treads in the fine, sandy particles." Armstrong would report that given the lack of gravity moving on the Moon was "even perhaps easier than the simulations...It's absolutely no trouble to walk around." Armstrong was so excited during his time on the Moon that his metabolic readings were worrying MOCR back on Earth, and they let him know about it.

Aldrin stepped out next onto the Moon, with a reminder from the MOCR to not lock the door, since the *Eagle* did not have a handle on the outside. Aldrin passed that test and made his own "small step for a man". He had now fulfilled his previous wish to join the "adventures" of the astronaut corps, going one step further onto another world, one he described for the ages as "magnificent desolation."[95] Aldrin later described the feeling:

> "Well, the first thing that I wanted to do when I got on the surface was to hold on and to just sort of bounce around and check the mobility that I had and then let go and see what the footing was like. All that took was maybe 30 seconds or a minute to feel that I knew how to move around with great confidence, and that's all the later crews really needed to do. So I was doing that for my benefit but for their benefit too. And later on in the spacewalk outside, when I jumped around and pranced around, again I was doing that for the benefit of the people back on Earth to see, and to measure what the mobility was like, so that it would give something in addition to our verbal description of observations when we got back. The things that we did on that first mission I felt were done to make later missions more successful. So we would look and see what the condition of the lander was, take pictures of it, so that later on the people wouldn't have to spend the time doing that. Our mission really was to put out some simple experiments: the laser reflector, the passive seismometer, to verify that the leveling devices and the antennas worked, to do some quick sampling of the surface. Because our lander was heavier than the later landers, we didn't have the room for the consumables, or the margin, to be able to stay out to go twice, for example, or to stay out even longer. Whatever the flight plan, and the engineers decided what our mission was going to be, and how many hours we could stay out, that was it; there wasn't any point in saying 'Well, hey, let's change that so instead of staying out two and a half hours, we can stay out four hours.' Gee, the guys did the calculations and they said that's what you could do, so that's what we stuck with."[96]

Armstrong Didn't Misspeak on the Moon. That's How Ohioans Talk," http://io9.com/neil-armstrong-didnt-misspeak-on-the-moon-thats-how-510920446
[95] "Ten Things You Didn't Know About the Apollo 11 Moon Landing," http://www.popsci.com/military-aviation-amp-space/article/2009-06/40-years-later-ten-things-you-didnt-know-about-apollo-ii-moon-landing
[96] "Buzz Aldrin," To the Moon, http://www.pbs.org/wgbh/nova/tothemoon/aldrin.html

**Aldrin's footprint on the Moon**

Armstrong made sure to collect a Moon sample as soon as possible in case they had to quickly abort the mission and return to Collins and the *Columbia*. Now Aldrin focused on the two activities he had "crammed" the hardest for: the collection of geologically important samples and the use of a camera to document lunar surface exploration. In this he was successful, though with one twist. Aldrin only captured three photos of Armstrong on the surface of the Moon; and most of those photos did not show Armstrong straight-on. The reason for this omission lay with the time the astronauts spent on the Moon, two-and-a-half hours. They might have spent most of their time on the most difficult task of all: pounding the U.S. flag into the ground and unfurling it.[97]

[97] *Rocket Men*, 279; Apollo 11: Lunar Surface Journal, http://www.hq.nasa.gov/alsj/a11/a11.html; "Why It's So Hard to Find Photos of Neil Armstrong on the Moon," http://io9.com/5938190/why-its-so-hard-to-find-photos-of-neil-armstrong-on-the-moon ; "The Missing Man: There are No Good Pictures of Neil Armstrong on the Moon," http://www.theatlantic.com/technology/archive/2012/08/the-missing-man-there-are-no-good-pictures-of-neil-armstrong-on-the-moon/261622/

**Armstrong's picture of Aldrin made sure to reflect the image of himself in Aldrin's visor**

The astronauts also took seismic readings of the surface, collected several pounds of rocks and samples, and left a plaque and other memorials at the landing site. The plaque read, "Here men from the planet Earth first set foot upon the Moon, July 1969 A.D. We came in peace for all mankind."

**Aldrin stands next to the Passive Seismic Experiment Package with the flag and the *Eagle* in the background**

## Chapter 9: Rendezvous

Armstrong and Aldrin entered the Ascent Stage with just enough time to take a phone call from President Richard M. Nixon, who told them:

> "Hello Neil and Buzz, I am talking to you by telephone from the Oval Room at the White House, and this certainly has to be the most historic telephone call ever made from the White House.

I just can't tell you how proud we all are of what you have done. For every American this has to be the proudest day of our lives, and for people all over the world I am sure that they, too, join with Americans in recognizing what an immense feat this is.

Because of what you have done the heavens have become a part of man's world, and as you talk to us from the Sea of Tranquility, it inspires us to redouble our efforts to bring peace and tranquility to earth.

For one priceless moment in the whole history of man all the people on this earth are truly one—one in their pride in what you have done and one in our prayers that you will return safely to earth."

Still, one more problem remained that called for a solution: the arm switch on the ascent engine had broken off. With a ballpoint pen, Aldrin fixed the switch, and the Ascent Stage that engineers feared would not separate performed exactly as designed. The Eagle had "wings" again, and the astronauts rocketed into lunar orbit.[98]

While Armstrong and Aldrin had walked on the Moon, the *Columbia* had remained in orbit with Collins, the forgotten man in many ways. For every revolution he and *Columbia* made behind the far side of the Moon, he was truly the "loneliest man in the world." Ironically, he also belonged to another unique group of people as one of the only people to not witness Armstrong's first steps on the Moon. With a lot of time spent in solitude, Collins contemplated his surroundings and the influence of the experience. During every revolution, when he could finally see the Earth again, alone against the sea of black and stars, he pondered its position and state: "From space there is no hint of ruggedness to the [the Earth]; smooth as a billiard ball, it seem delicately poised on its circular journey around the Sun, and above all it seems fragile. Is the sea water clean enough to pour over your head, or is there a glaze of oil on its surface?...Is the riverbank a delight or an obscenity? The difference between a blue-and-white planet and a black-and-brown one is delicate indeed."[99]

As he stayed in orbit, he wrote, "I am alone now, truly alone, and absolutely isolated from any known life. I'm it...I feel this powerfully -- not as fear or loneliness -- but as awareness, anticipation, satisfaction, confidence, almost exultation. I like the feeling."[100]

That said, meditations and connecting with the universe should not suggest that Collins had nothing to do in orbit or nothing to worry about. At one point, a problem developed with the coolant system on the *Columbia*, a situation that put Collins on edge. He solved that problem, but

---

[98] *Rocket Men*, 281.
[99] *Rocket Men*, 275.
[100] *Rocket Men*, 289.

he still faced a bigger problem. The location of the *Eagle* on the Moon remained a mystery; and no one at NASA knew exactly where it had landed either. This could have meant trouble for the rendezvous between the two craft.

**Picture of the *Eagle's* ascent stage heading toward *Columbia***

Since the Moon has no atmosphere, it was relatively easy for the *Eagle* to ascend without needing powerful rockets like the Saturn V. It only required the Ascent Stage with fuel propulsion engines to propel it back up to the *Columbia*, and once they linked back up, the ascent stage was jettisoned into orbit, eventually landing back on the Moon. The ascent was not without its issues either. One of the enduring images of the Apollo 11 mission was the planting of the American flag on the Moon's surface. Since the Moon has no atmosphere, there is no wind on the surface. Thus, the flag needed to be specially designed to remain completely unfurled. And with no wind on the surface, the intent was to have the flag stand forever. However, the mission's planners had overlooked one important detail. In one of the most unreported (and forgotten) aspects of the Apollo 11 mission, the ascent of the *Eagle* off the Moon's surface generated enough wind to inadvertently blow the flag over during liftoff. Aldrin watched the flag blow over and mentioned it during the ascent, making NASA aware of the issue. He later explained, "The ascent stage of the LM separated... I was concentrating on the computers, and Neil was studying the attitude indicator, but I looked up long enough to see the flag fall over." As a result, the astronauts on all subsequent Apollo missions made sure to plant the flag much farther away from the lunar module to avoid Apollo 11's mistake.

Collins could only look through the sextant and wait to sight the *Eagle*. He finally did, and after a complicated series of events to get the two ports to line up and hard dock, the latches clicked into place, and the *Eagle* and *Columbia* were reunited. The hatch was opened, and laughing and cheering began. Collins remembered the moment of reunion: "[I] grabbed Buzz by both ears and I was gonna kiss him on the forehead, I can remember that, and I got him to right about here and I said 'Eh, this is not a good thing to do somehow,' and I forgot, I clapped him on the back or shook his hand or something."[101]

## Chapter 10: The Trip Home

The Moon's orbit is only a fraction of Earth's, so once the modules linked back up, the *Columbia* module was equipped with engines to propel it back toward Earth. The bigger concern for the return was that the modules had to reenter Earth's orbit at the proper angle to allow the planet to recapture it. Reentry into Earth's atmosphere subjects spacecrafts to temperatures of about 3,000 degrees Fahrenheit, so the module had an elaborate heat shield consisting of a mixture of dozens of panels, insulation and aluminum. A failure in any part of the heat shield system would be fatal.

As Apollo 11 made its way back to Earth, the astronauts broadcast one last time on July 23 and gave thanks to everyone involved. Collins told the audience, "The Saturn V rocket which put us in orbit is an incredibly complicated piece of machinery, every piece of which worked flawlessly ... We have always had confidence that this equipment will work properly. All this is possible only through the blood, sweat, and tears of a number of a people ...All you see is the three of us, but beneath the surface are thousands and thousands of others, and to all of those, I would like to say, 'Thank you very much.'"

Likewise, Aldrin told viewers, "This has been far more than three men on a mission to the Moon; more, still, than the efforts of a government and industry team; more, even, than the efforts of one nation. We feel that this stands as a symbol of the insatiable curiosity of all

---

[101] *Rocket Men*, 298.

mankind to explore the unknown ... Personally, in reflecting on the events of the past several days, a verse from Psalms comes to mind. 'When I consider the heavens, the work of Thy fingers, the Moon and the stars, which Thou hast ordained; What is man that Thou art mindful of him?'"

Armstrong said, ""The responsibility for this flight lies first with history and with the giants of science who have preceded this effort; next with the American people, who have, through their will, indicated their desire; next with four administrations and their Congresses, for implementing that will; and then, with the agency and industry teams that built our spacecraft, the Saturn, the Columbia, the Eagle, and the little EMU, the spacesuit and backpack that was our small spacecraft out on the lunar surface. We would like to give special thanks to all those Americans who built the spacecraft; who did the construction, design, the tests, and put their hearts and all their abilities into those craft. To those people tonight, we give a special thank you, and to all the other people that are listening and watching tonight, God bless you. Good night from Apollo 11."

Finally, it was time for the splashdown. The module had several "drogue parachutes," used for decelerating fast moving objects, which were used at about 25,000 feet. Those parachutes slowed the module down to about 125 miles per hour. Another set of parachutes would then slow the module down to about 20 miles per hour before it hit the water. Once the module splashed down, divers would deploy rafts to pick up the astronauts and anchor the module while a helicopter hovered overhead to collect everyone and everything. After being picked up, the returning astronauts would be quarantined for a period of time to study the effects the mission had on their bodies.

**The splashdown of the *Columbia***

On July 24, Apollo 11 headed back to Earth and the splashdown in the Pacific Ocean, and the men would spend nearly a month in biological quarantine just to be careful. NASA had created an extensive but flawed process to protect the Earth from possible "Moon germs," but in the end the men would return home. Of course, their lives were never the same, and all three would leave NASA and the astronaut corps by the middle of the 1970s.

**President Nixon visits the quarantined astronauts**

### Chapter 1!: The Aftermath of Apollo 11

Apollo 11 may be the most famous space mission in history, but NASA only intended for it to be the first of many manned missions to the Moon. Within four months of Apollo 11's mission, Apollo 12 sat on the launch pad, ready to go to the Moon for a more extended duration. Apollo 12 is largely forgotten today, sandwiched between the two most famous Apollo missions, but it was actually one of the most successful Apollo missions. Although Apollo 11 was an obvious success, the mission encountered some problems, particularly the *Eagle's* descent to the Moon's surface. Apollo 12's mission was designed to correct the kinks, while also staying on the Moon longer to conduct more sophisticated experiments.

Apollo 12 landed on the Moon's surface using cutting edge Doppler radar, and almost all of the lunar module's descent was done automatically, both improvements over Apollo 11. Apollo 12 made a near perfect landing in the "Ocean of Storms," chosen because NASA knew its earlier unmanned probe, Surveyor 3, had landed there two years earlier. NASA wanted Apollo 12's crew to collect the probe's parts and bring them back for analysis. Apollo 12's crew also took more samples, tested the Moon's magnetic field, and set up instruments that would continue to transmit data to Earth long after the mission.

Apollo 13 likely would have faded into relative obscurity had it successfully completed its mission, because that has largely been Apollo 14's fate. Apollo 14 successfully analyzed the Fra Mauro highlands and crater by spending over 30 hours on the Moon's surface. Apollo 14 also debuted the "Modularized Equipment Transporter," a fancy name for what was essentially the Moon's first wheelbarrow. It allowed the astronauts to lug nearly 100 pounds of equipment and samples around on the surface. One of these astronauts was Alan Shepard, Jr., who a decade earlier had become the first American in space aboard Freedom 7.

Apollo 14 may have used the first vehicle on the Moon, but Apollo 15 trumped it on July 30, 1971, when it landed on the Moon with the Moon's first rover. Unbeknownst to the United States, the Soviets had put a tiny rover aboard Mars 3 and launched it toward Mars just two months earlier, but Apollo 15's Lunar Roving Vehicle was the first rover to land on another celestial body.

The Lunar Roving Vehicle became a staple of photographs and video shot during the final Apollo missions, and they are instantly recognizable today. The rover could travel about 10 miles per hour, allowing the crew to travel greater distances more easily in their bulky suits. Apollo 15's astronauts covered several miles on each rover, as did the astronauts of Apollo 16 and 17. All three rovers were left behind on the Moon's surface.

On the way back to Earth, Apollo 15 had the distinction of being the first mission to leave a satellite in Moon's orbit, allowing NASA to analyze the Moon's magnetic field, among other measurements. But Apollo 15 had been the fourth manned mission to land on the Moon in two years, and, at least to outside observers like President Nixon, each mission was accomplishing less noteworthy things. Except for the drama of Apollo 13, the missions never recaptured the original excitement of the first lunar landing mission, so it was only natural Apollo experienced a letdown. As the public's interest waned, missions were canceled, and the complete vision of the "Apollo Applications Project" would never be realized except for Skylab, the first and only American space station, which was fittingly launched by a Saturn V rocket.[102]

Less than a month after Apollo 15's mission, the Nixon Administration began pressuring NASA to pull the plug on the remaining Apollo missions. NASA had actually started doing the budget math nearly a year before Apollo 15 launched. In September 1970, NASA canceled two planned Apollo missions. But NASA was still able to launch Apollo 16 and Apollo 17 in 1972, with both missions placing an emphasis on the Moon's geology. Apollo 16 looked for volcanic

---

[102] *Rocket Men*, 30, 303; Google Moon, "Apollo Series," http://www.google.com/moon/; "Apollo 18: The Lost Apollo Missions," http://news.discovery.com/space/the-lost-apollo-missions-110902.htm;

activity among the Moon's highlands, while Apollo 17's crew included a professional geologist. On December 14, 1972, Apollo 17 Commander Eugene A. Cernan stepped off the Moon and back into the lunar module. No man has set foot on the Moon since.

Apollo 17 was the last Apollo mission. NASA ended up canceling three Apollo missions, designated today as Apollo 18, 19 and 20 even though two of those missions were to occur before Apollo 17. These missions were canceled due to budget cuts, and the materials for Apollo 20 were instead used for the Skylab, America's first space station.

By the end of the Apollo program, NASA had already begun designing and developing the Space Shuttle Program, which would provide reusable vehicles for manned space travel and theoretically save money.

A number of reasons explain why the U.S. succeeded and sent astronauts to the Moon. Each of the men who flew on those missions represented the best parts of the nation's efforts and willingness to make the sacrifice. The success may have been best described by the then-director of NASA, James E. Webb. He left office before Apollo 11's triumph, but his captured the essence of what made the Apollo program such a uniquely American success:

> "The nations of the world, seeking a basis for their own futures, continually pass judgment of our ability as a nation to make decisions, to concentrate effort, to manage vast and complex technological programs in our interest. It is not too much to say that in many ways the viability of representative government and of the free enterprise system in a period of revolutionary changes based on science and technology is being tested in space...[Society has] reached a point where its progress and even its survival increasingly depend upon our ability to organize the complex and do the unusual. We cannot do these things except through large aggregations of resources and power. [It is] revolution from above."[103]

Some have pointed out that the success of Apollo 11 and the program as a whole is made all the more remarkable by the fact that changes in society over time might preclude similar results. As one group of British scientists commemorating the 40th anniversary noted, "It was carried out in a technically brilliant way with risks taken... that would be inconceivable in the risk-averse world of today... The Apollo programme is arguably the greatest technical achievement of mankind to date... nothing since Apollo has come close [to] the excitement that was generated by those astronauts - Armstrong, Aldrin and the 10 others who followed them."

---

[103] *Rocket Men*, 177.

**Picture of the *Columbia* at the Smithsonian National Air & Space Museum**

42674368R00040

Made in the USA
Middletown, DE
16 April 2019